What

MW00398041

BLOOD ON THE DOOR

"The Kingdom of God is manifested in our lives through purpose, design and structure. We see these truths throughout the scriptures from Genesis to Revelation, in the creation of the heavens and the earth as well as mankind.

Over the years, books have been written that gave insight into how purpose, design, and structure are made operational in the believer's life—books such as P.C. Nelson's *Bible Doctrines*, Ralph Riggs' *The Spirit Himself*, and Oral Roberts' *Miracle of Seed Faith*. That is why I am excited by *Blood on the Door*. It is a book written to equip the believer to create a lifestyle of victory.

Ted Shuttlesworth Jr. has reached back to a foundation stone that has been pushed aside and, in some cases, forgotten. He not only reminds us of the relevance of the blood of Jesus; he reveals its everlasting power! This is not just a must-read book—it is a foundation stone."

— RICK THOMAS, bishop, Abundant Life Church, Margate, FL; author of *Significant Seed Perpetual Harvest* and *Capturing the Mind of God*

"In *Blood on the Door*, Ted Shuttlesworth Jr. gives us truths that, considering the hour in which we live, are vital for every believer. The blood cleanses, washes, purifies, delivers, empowers, equips, and protects.

The Church needs to know the power that's available to them in and through the blood of Christ. Remember, Hebrews 2:3 reads, "How shall we escape, if we neglect so great salvation?" Apply these truths in your life today."

— DR. RODNEY HOWARD-BROWNE, pastor, The River Church, Tampa, FL; author of *Seeing Jesus as He Really Is* and *The Touch of God*

"Join my good friend Ted Shuttlesworth Jr. as he unpacks the powerful revelation of Christ's blood shed for you. His joyful yet deeply spiritual style will inspire your faith and empower you to triumph in every area of your Christian walk."

— JOEL STOCKSTILL, director, Bethany Influence, Dallas, TX; author of *Faith that Endures* and *Power of Daily Bible Reading*

"*Blood on the Door* sizzles with illuminating imagery casting truth over the shadows of doubt and unbelief. Ted's writing brings a new perspective to the timeless illustrations found in the Word of God. This book abounds with truth for a fresh impartation and is truly inspired by the Holy Spirit."

—STEVEN MCCARTT, pastor, Family Worship Center, Florence, SC

"Ted has taken a subject that many people are not talking about today and has made it the very thing that everyone should be talking about. Full of revelation and truth, *Blood on the Door* beautifully illuminates the power of the blood of Christ, what His blood has purchased for every child of God, how it is to be applied, and how to walk in this covenant every day."

—ALAN MUSHEGAN, pastor, Full Turn Church, Hiram, GA; author of *On Purpose* and *Heir of Power*

Also by Ted Shuttlesworth Jr.

Praise. Laugh. Repeat: Living in the Power
of Overwhelming Joy

Praise. Laugh. Repeat. Devotional: A 40-Day Journey
to Overwhelming Joy

BLOOD
ON THE DOOR

*The Protective Power
of Covenant*

TED SHUTTLESWORTH JR.

MIRACLE WORD
PUBLISHING

Published in Virginia Beach, Virginia by Miracle Word Publishing.

Miracle Word titles may be purchased in bulk for educational, business, fundraising, or sales promotional use. For information, please e-mail info@miracle-word.com

Unless otherwise indicated, all Scripture quotations are taken from the Holy Bible, New Living Translation, copyright © 1996, 2004, 2007, 2013 by Tyndale House Foundation. Used by permission of Tyndale House Publishers, Inc., Carol Stream, Illinois 60188. All rights reserved.

Scripture quotations are from the ESV® Bible (The Holy Bible, English Standard Version®), copyright © 2001 by Crossway, a publishing ministry of Good News Publishers. Used by permission. All rights reserved.

Scripture quotations marked KJV are from THE KING JAMES VERSION of the Bible, public domain.

Scripture quotations marked NKJV are from the NEW KING JAMES VERSION. © 1982 by Thomas Nelson, Inc. Used by permission. All rights reserved.

Scripture quotations marked NASB are taken from the New American Standard Bible®, Copyright © 1960, 1962, 1963, 1968, 1971, 1972, 1973, 1975, 1977, 1995 by The Lockman Foundation Used by permission." (www.Lockman.org)

Scripture quotations marked AMP are taken from the Amplified Bible, Copyright © 1954, 1958, 1962, 1964, 1965, 1987 by The Lockman Foundation. Used by permission.

Scripture quotations from THE MESSAGE. Copyright © by Eugene H. Peterson 1993, 1994, 1995, 1996, 2000, 2001, 2002. Used by permission of NavPress. All rights reserved. Represented by Tyndale House Publishers, Inc.

All uppercase text in verses of scripture are added by the author for the purpose of emphasis.

ISBN 978-0-9909196-3-6

Printed in the United States of America

For Carolyn, my best friend.
You've made ten years feel like ten minutes.
I love you eternally.

CONTENTS

FOREWORD

*This charge I commit unto thee, son Timothy, according to the
prophecies which went before on thee, that thou by them
mightest war a good warfare;*
—1 TIMOTHY 1:18 KJV

There are certain men that the Lord has used to teach
and reinforce sound doctrine in every generation. A
multitude of men and women have been used to speak
and influence their generation. We need men and wom-
en to speak the Word of God today.

One of those men is my son. My wife and I traveled
with our children from the day they were born until
they left home to follow the will of God. I remember
placing my son on the front rows of churches and tents
so I could keep my eye on him, and there he sat in the
presence of the Lord.

God was performing miracles in one of our meetings
and I was praying for a woman who had a large goiter
in her neck. When I laid hands on her, the growth disappeared. My four-year-old son jumped up in excitement
and yelled, "Do it again, Dad!"

When you are raised in an atmosphere of the precious

anointing of the Holy Spirit, something takes place in the human heart or spirit.

The Lord allowed me to work closely with a great man of God, R.W. Schambach. He introduced me to other wonderful men and women of God like T. L. Osborn, Lester Sumrall, Kenneth Hagin, John Osteen, and Frieda Lindsay. That my son and daughter were able to be around anointed ministers and receive from them was a great encouragement to me and my wife.

Impartation is real, and I am not surprised that Teddy received a call from the Lord. Many times I have talked to him about how God gave a signature theme to His ministers.

Blood on the Door is a much-needed voice for help and deliverance to this generation. "And it shall come to pass, that whosoever shall call on the name of the Lord shall be saved" (Acts 2:21).

The Blood must be applied, but then there is an open door to the benefits that Christ has provided. When you find out what belongs to you as a child of God in this book, you will live a life of victory!

Ted Shuttlesworth Sr.
Hill Cottage, West Virginia
March 2016

PREFACE

I am leaving you with a gift — peace of mind and heart. And the
peace I give is a gift the world cannot give.
So don't be troubled or afraid.
—JOHN 14:27 NLT

I was sitting in class on a normal Tuesday morning in 2001 (probably trying to stay awake since I'm not a morning person), when an announcement came over the college's intercom.

We were told that a tragedy had occurred, and all students were to leave their classes and proceed immediately to the auditorium of the church.

Now I was really awake.

As the crowd of students proceeded along the sidewalk, some were receiving calls and texts about what happened. Two large planes had flown into the World Trade Center, causing the buildings to collapse, and killing almost 3,000 people.

After we entered the church and received the full announcement, we prayed for the nation for over an hour. Many paced the auditorium with tears in their eyes, asking God to touch our country.

Something changed in America after 9/11. Nine days later, during a televised address to a joint session of congress, President Bush declared that America was now engaged in a *war on terror.*[1]

Terror.

How do you fight against a feeling? Since then, it seems that feeling has intensified in America and around the world.

Whether it's 9/11, viral outbreaks of disease, the economic downturn of 2008, breaking news about groups like al-Qaeda, Boko Haram, and ISIS, school shootings, natural disasters that seem to be escalating around the world, or attacks like we saw in Paris and Brussels, the hearts of people seem to be filled with *terror.*

The more I saw this around our nation and other nations, I felt a burden from the Lord to write this book. Should Christians be worried as the days grow darker before the coming of the Lord? Is there hope and protection for God's people?

I believe there is.

This book will guide you through the Word of God and reveal how to access the protective power of "the shadow of the Almighty" (Psalm 91).

As Jesus said, *"Don't be troubled or afraid."*

THE NIGHT THE CHILDREN DIED

*"Something is coming. Jehovah is sending an angel. A . . .
death angel," he grimaced. "It's coming tonight."*
— *Jabari to Adriel hours before the first Passover*

EGYPT, 1313 BC

Seventh hour of the day.

The whip came down with a loud *CRACK!* Someone in
front of Adriel shrieked in pain as the braided leather
snapped across the skin of his bare back.

Adriel took a deep breath, straining to fill his lungs
with the thick, humid air that permeated the Egyptian
terrain, and then spit several wandering gnats from his
mouth.

He kept his eyes down as he worked, not wanting
to be singled out by the Egyptian taskmasters. Beads of
sweat fell from his face and dotted the sandy ground
around his sandals.

More than ever, Adriel and the other slaves were being pushed to produce more clay bricks each day than

seemed possible. The harder they worked, the harder they were driven. The taskmasters were cruel, but Adriel could press through most days . . . unless Ammon and his son were there.

Adriel prayed to Jehovah each day that Pharaoh would have another assignment for Ammon that would keep him from coming to inspect the work of the Hebrews.

Ammon was a leader among the taskmasters. His heavily-muscled frame towered above the others. His eyes contained pure evil, and in them Adriel could see the harsh contempt Ammon had for the people of God.

Every slave prayed that Ammon would not come. Although bigger than anyone, he would arrive unseen and move about like a ghost.

His whip, *Serket*, meaning scorpion, was known and feared throughout every tribe. Small, sharpened pieces of metal had been attached to the ends of the braided leather. The frail, bony bodies of the Jewish slaves were no match for the brutal lashings from the giant Egyptian. If Ammon was angry and got carried away, it could mean death for his victim.

His eldest son, Odion, was no different. Although he was a young teenager and not as massive as his father, Odion was just as hateful and cruel.

Ammon's eyes would glow with pride as he would

watch Odion stalk through the crowd of Hebrews and deal out lashes with his own whip when he thought the slaves were slacking. *Following in his father's footsteps,* Adriel thought.

"Adriel!" The hissing whisper snapped him out of his daydreams. He turned to see his friend, Jabari, working next to him. "This Moses is going to get us all killed," he said with fear in his eyes.

"Keep your voice down," Adriel said, stealing a quick glance at the closest taskmasters.

"Trust me, I would rather be whipped than killed," Jabari whispered, returning his eyes to his work. "Aren't you worried about your son?"

For a moment, Adriel could feel his heart beating heavily as apprehension overtook him. His son, Benjamin, was all he had left in the world. His wife had died during childbirth and now that Benjamin was old enough to work among the slave men, Adriel was more worried than ever.

Jabari was right. It was odd that Moses had instructed the Hebrew slaves to ask their Egyptian neighbors for their gold and silver. Stranger still, the Egyptians had given it to them without even a question.

It must be a mistake, a trap, Adriel concluded. He dreaded what would happen once the Egyptians realized what they had done.

How foolish for a slave's home to be filled with valuable gold and silver. With the expensive possessions piled next to their broken clay pots and flasks, something felt out of place.

"Don't worry. Jehovah will protect us," Adriel said softly. His voice barely rose above a whisper.

"I hope for Benjamin's sake you're right," Jabari mumbled into the pile of bricks at his knees.

Adriel looked over to where his son Benjamin was working and his heart immediately sank. Twenty meters away, a solid tower of muscle drifted across the desert floor as silence fell over the crowd.

Ammon.

His dark, braided goatee outlined the yellow teeth of his vicious smirk. A steady *clink-clink* penetrated the silence as *Serket's* metal tips danced at Ammon's side tapping his shiny body armor.

Keep your head down, my son. Be silent and tend to your bricks, Adriel thought. Normally, this might have worked. Ammon usually harassed the older men. He claimed they were challenging his authority. He made them answer for it.

But he wasn't alone.

Odion pranced forward from behind his father, swinging his whip in a circle. He relished the opportunity to use it whenever he could.

Ten meters.

Odion was spewing insults in every direction as his father smiled a cold, unforgiving smile.

"This is the laziest pack of mongrels I've ever seen," Odion spat. A pitiful howl rang out as he snapped his whip into the skin of the nearest slave.

Even the other taskmasters looked uneasy when Ammon and Odion arrived. It was as though they thought Ammon might even turn on them if the occasion presented itself. They were probably right.

Five meters.

"Who is this little man?" Odion's voice dripped with sarcasm as it echoed through the crowd.

Please, God, no.

Adriel looked up to see Odion standing over young Benjamin with his whip hand on his waist.

"You don't look like much of a man. A baby perhaps?" Odion asked with his eyebrows raised.

"Y-yes, s-s-sir," Benjamin stuttered, not raising his eyes from Odion's sandals. His body began to shake in fear.

"Sir? You refuse to call me master?" Odion's brow descended into a mountain, casting shadow over his deep-sunk eyes.

"Maybe a few lashes will remind you of your position, dog," he said as he grabbed Benjamin by the arm.

He pulled him to his feet.

Adriel's body tensed and he quickly began to stand. A strong hand yanked him back down to his knees.

"Don't, Adriel!" Jabari hissed, his eyes widened. "It will be worse for you . . . and for Benjamin."

Benjamin cried out in fear as the bigger boy dragged his body across the sand toward the whipping post.

Adriel realized that Jabari was still holding his arm tightly as they watched Odion yank Benjamin to his feet again. He had lost a sandal in the struggle toward the post and stood on one bare foot.

"Papa!" Benjamin cried as his eyes frantically searched the crowd of slaves who were watching solemnly.

He can't see me. Adriel realized.

The last word uttered by his son caused a surge of strength and energy to flow through Adriel's body. He ripped his arm away from Jabari's grasp and leapt to his feet.

"Adriel, no!" Jabari said, but Adriel barely heard a sound. He began to run through the crowd at full speed. With the attention of the slaves and taskmasters on Odion and Benjamin, no one realized what was happening until it was too late.

He passed the last row of slaves and broke into the open. Taskmasters began to shout as they saw him emerge.

Adriel hurdled the last few strides and flung his body full force into Odion, knocking him into the dirt. Odion snarled in frustration as he rolled over onto his back in a daze.

Benjamin stood free at the whipping post, looking at his father with tears in his eyes.

"Papa," he whispered as the wetness of a tear cut through the dirt on his cheek.

"Run, my son!" Adriel commanded. "Run and hide."

Benjamin turned and fled. Newfound strength seemed to fill his little legs as Adriel watched him disappear.

"Sieze him!" Guards and taskmasters rushed forward and pinned Adriel to the ground. Others attempted to chase after Benjamin, but he was long gone.

"Let the boy go," boomed a voice above Adriel. "He will be found easily enough." Ammon sneered down at Adriel.

"I will enjoy this, dog."

Odion had recovered his senses and had come back to his feet. He now stood enraged behind his father.

"Kill him!" He screamed. "Kill that piece of filth!"

"He will wish I had killed him," Ammon said. Adriel heard the metallic *clink-clink* as Ammon unravelled *Serket* from his belt.

Second Watch of the night.

Adriel opened his eyes. It was dark and everything a blur. He closed them again. The strong smell of garlic and spiced lamb caused him to wake more fully.

He heard a fire crackling in the small hearth of his one-room house as he tried to focus.

He turned his head to see Jabari kneeling beside the fire, turning a thick piece of mutton on a spit over the flames. There was a hiss as the grease dripped onto the glowing coals below.

Adriel groaned, rolling onto his side. Jabari's head turned quickly from the flames and he rushed to the side of the bed.

"My friend, I didn't know if you'd wake again after what happened." Adriel shut his eyes tightly trying to remember. Then it flooded back like a nightmare.

Serket. Ammon. The searing pain . . . and the laughter. That awful, booming laughter.

"If Ammon had not been summoned by Pharaoh," Jabari continued, "I fear you would be dead."

Adriel attempted to sit up, but fell back to his pillow as waves of burning pain shot through the muscles of his back and legs.

Jabari watched him with a furrowed brow. "You must not move, my friend. You need rest." He pressed his hands against Adriel's chest and pulled a blanket around him as though he expected Adriel to protest.

A growl rumbled from Adriel's stomach as the smell of the fresh meat took effect. He hadn't eaten since the previous night's dinner and he was famished.

"I have news for you, Adriel," Jabari said, pacing back to the hearth. "The elders have given us instruction from Moses."

"What news?"

"We're leaving. Leaving for good," Jabari said, but the look in his eyes betrayed him.

He doesn't even believe what he's saying.

"Just like that? Pharaoh is letting us leave? Are you mad?" Adriel wanted to believe but couldn't. Slaves are slaves for life.

"While you slept I received word from the elders. Very specific, too. Very specific." He tossed some bitter greens into a pan and drizzled oil over the top of them.

Looking down, Adriel saw that Jabari had even prepared flat bread on the stones by the fire.

"I've never known you to be a cook, Jabari," Adriel said with an eyebrow raised.

"Part of the instructions we received," he said quickly. "We're to eat this lamb, the greens, and the bread and not leave any leftovers. We must eat it fully clothed and with our walking sticks close by."

Adriel noticed that Jabari had already dressed him

and put his sandals on his feet. Adriel's walking staff was leaning against the corner by his bed.

"There's something else," Jabari said, his tone turning instantly darker. He looked at Adriel, but it was an empty gaze as though Jabari was staring into space imagining something. "Something is coming."

Adriel raised himself on one elbow. "What do you mean, something is coming?"

"Moses says Jehovah is sending an angel. A . . . *death angel*," he grimaced. "It's coming tonight."

For a moment the only sound in the small home was the sizzling of the meat cooking on the spit. Adriel considered what he'd just heard.

"A death angel," Adriel repeated.

"That's what this is for." Jabari walked to the wooden table in the middle of the room and gestured to a large pot. He dipped his finger in and held it to show Adriel.

The firelight glinted off of the shiny, red liquid running down his finger.

"It's the blood of the lamb," Jabari said softly nodding toward the fire. "Moses says that we must use it to mark the doorpost of our home. It will serve as a signal. When the death angel sees the blood on the door, he will know the people living there belong to the Lord and he will pass over that house. If not . . ."

"He will kill everyone inside?" Adriel finished.

"Not everyone, just the firstborn sons."

Adriel's heart began to pound in his chest as he jerked his head around the room.

"Where's Benjamin? Where's my son?" He said returning his eyes to his friend. Jabari dropped his gaze to the floor as he answered.

"He . . . he hasn't returned. I've not seen him since he ran off this afternoon."

Adriel ignored the pain and threw the blanket from his body and swung his legs out of bed.

"You knew this was happening and you haven't gone to find Benjamin?" Adriel stumbled to his feet, knocking his walking stick onto the dusty floor.

"People are searching, Adriel," Jabari protested. "Friends, neighbors."

Lord, be with him, Adriel prayed silently. He picked his staff up from the floor and moved toward the door.

"You must not go, you need strength."

"This is the life of my son! My Benjamin!" He realized love gave him strength that Jabari could not understand. "I will find him and bring him back. Prepare the house."

He opened the door and disappeared into the night.

Second Watch of the night.
Adriel collapsed against a stone wall that lined the dusty

streets of the city. He had been searching for his son for over an hour and a half but could find no sign of him.

His chest heaved vigorously as he tried to catch his breath and regain some strength. His shirt, which was little more than a rag, was drenched with the blood of his open wounds.

He jerked forward and grimaced as his damaged skin and muscles throbbed. Pieces of flesh hung open where *Serket's* metal tips had torn his back apart.

I must press on. I must find my son.

Adriel bowed his head and began to pray. "Please guide me, Jehovah. Bring me to my Benjamin."

A small cloud of dust rose into the air as Adriel dropped onto the ground. He bowed his head, clutched his hair tightly, and began to weep.

The streets surrounding him, which were a bustle of activity during the day, had fallen relatively quiet. Everyone was tucked inside their homes for the night.

Adriel could smell a fish roasting nearby. Someone was preparing for a late-night snack.

Fish!

That was it. How could he not think to check the secluded cove on the banks of the Nile that he and Benjamin had discovered a few years ago?

It had become their personal sanctuary. When the opportunity presented itself, he and his son would spend time hidden inside the cove while fishing the banks of the great river. They had never spoken of its location.

"He must be there," Adriel mumbled excitedly. He glanced up at the moon and realized it was almost midnight . . . and that's when he saw it.

Something passed in front of the moon. It couldn't be a falling star, it was moving too slowly. It was . . . descending.

Adriel squinted and followed the shape as it approached the ground. Even from a great distance he was able to make out a few details.

Outstretched arms. A head. It's a person.

It landed on the main street running through the center of the city. Although hundreds of meters away, Adriel could now see it clearly.

A large figure cloaked in black began to slowly pace down the street. Finally, Adriel watched as it slowed in front of the first house to which it came.

Oh, God, no. Not yet. Please.

Moses was right. The Death Angel had come just as Jehovah said he would. The dark figure reached out his arm and seemed to touch the door frame of the house.

That's when the screams began and Adriel realized he was out of time. He began to run.

To be continued . . .

REDEMPTION IS NOT A PACKAGE OF PROMISES; IT IS A COLLECTION OF COVENANT TERMS.

PART 1

HOW TO PAINT
YOUR DOOR

YOUR LIFE SHOULDN'T LOOK THE SAME AS SOMEONE WHO DOESN'T HAVE A REDEEMER.

CHAPTER 1

THE DANGER OF CLEAN DOORS

But the blood on your doorposts will serve as a sign, marking the houses where you are staying. When I see the blood, I will pass over you. This plague of death will not touch you when I strike the land of Egypt.
—EXODUS 12:13 NLT

My plane touched down at the Hartsfield-Jackson Airport in Atlanta, Georgia. I was on my way to Kingston, Jamaica, to preach for two weeks.

I grabbed my carry-on baggage and got off the plane. As I was walking through the terminal, I noticed a few people wearing light-blue surgical masks.

Weird. I'd occasionally seen people wearing them—allergies, I'd assumed—but I'd never seen groups wearing masks. Definitely not as many as I was seeing today.

I started wondering what was going on. I thought of the Dustin Hoffman movie *Outbreak*, with the monkey that was spreading a virus through the population of California.

I subtly scanned the terminal for crazed monkeys

roaming the halls. Needless to say, it was all clear.

Later, I found out that an Ebola outbreak in West Africa had sickened over 14,000 people and killed over 5,000 since that March.

Six months later, in September, a man from Liberia came to the United States to visit his family and became one of the first people since the outbreak to be diagnosed with Ebola on U.S. soil. He later died at the Texas Health Presbyterian Hospital in Dallas.

It was now November, and more cases had been reported in the United States. People were clearly afraid.

I later saw an ABC News headline that read: "Ebola in America," and detailed the story of what had taken place. As I read the article, there was a portion that stood out as though it were highlighted in yellow. It read:

> Another person has died of Ebola on American soil, reminding U.S. citizens that although many health workers have survived the virus, even treatment at one of the best facilities doesn't guarantee being cured.[1]

That struck a chord in my heart. Now I could understand the people's fear. They were doing their best not to catch the virus. They realized that if they did, hospitals may not even be able to help them.

This is a thought that raises a question in the mind of every human being. *What do you do when there is no doctor who can help you?* What of the diseases like cancer for which we have no cure?

In her book, *A World without Cancer*, Dr. Margaret Cuomo (sister of New York Governor Andrew Cuomo) included some statistics regarding cancer research:

> More than 40 years after the war on cancer was declared, we have spent billions fighting the good fight. The National Cancer Institute has spent some $90 billion on research and treatment during that time. Some 260 nonprofit organizations in the United States have dedicated themselves to cancer — more than the number established for heart disease, AIDS, Alzheimer's disease, and stroke combined. Together, these 260 organizations have budgets that top $2.2 billion.[2]

She goes on to state that although there have been some small declines in common cancers since the early 1990s, "cancer's role in one out of every four deaths in this country remains a haunting statistic."[3]

It seems like our help cannot come from men. I'm not against hospitals or doctors, but there comes a time when there's nothing else they can do for us. That fact is as true today as it was in the days of Jesus.

> *A woman in the crowd had suffered for twelve years with constant bleeding. She had suffered a great deal from many doctors, and over the years she had spent everything she had to pay them, but she had gotten no better. In fact, she had gotten worse.*
>
> *Mark 5:25-26 NLT*

The reason this story has a happy ending is because that woman in the Bible came to a realization: *Men can't help me. My help must come from a supernatural source.*

She realized that Jesus was able to do for her in one moment what doctors could not do in many years. Faith puts its trust in God alone.

It's not just foolish for us to put our trust in humans who are imperfect, it's also dangerous.

The prophet Jeremiah gave correction to the people of Israel who had stopped worshiping and serving God. They had also stopped trusting in God, which resulted in His anger. He was frustrated because like any loving father, He wanted to give gifts to His children and bless them. However, because God can only interact with His children through faith, their lack of faith caused their blessing to slip through their fingers.

Jeremiah issued them a warning from the Lord:

> *Cursed are those who put their trust in mere humans, who rely on human strength and turn their hearts away from the Lord. They are like stunted shrubs in the desert, with no hope for the future.*
>
> *Jeremiah 17:5-6 NLT*

Bishop David Oyedepo is the pastor of one of the world's largest churches, Winner's Chapel. The church is located in Ota, Nigeria, where they host five packed Sunday morning services in their 55,000-seat auditorium. His ministry was built by total dependency on God.

In 1983, while in a prayer session with members of his staff, the Lord asked him a humorous question.

"My son, you have two eyes; can you make one to look up and the other to look down?" He tried it and answered, "No." Then God said to him, "Any time you are looking unto man, never claim you are looking unto me."[4] Then the Lord reminded him of a Scripture:

> *They looked to Him and were radiant, And their faces will never be ashamed.*
>
> *Psalm 34:5 NASB*

God never wants to see His children hurting or in bondage. In fact, from Genesis to Revelation we have stories of God creating ways to deliver His people from danger and oppression.

DIRTY DOORS

The book of Exodus is a story of God raising up a man named Moses as a deliverer to bring the children of Israel out of bondage.

The Jews had been slaves in Egypt for hundreds of years, but God had a plan to free them. Moses and Aaron stood before Pharaoh and commanded that he let God's people go. The hardness of Pharaoh's heart caused God to send ten plagues as judgments upon the Egyptian people.

It's very important to note that the Jews (God's people) were not affected by the plagues (Exodus 8:23). The Old Testament is filled with stories that act as examples — theologians call these "types and shadows" — of things that would happen in the New Testament.

For example, in this story, Pharaoh holding the Jews in slavery is an example of Satan who was holding God's people in the bondage of sin. Moses is a type of Christ who came as a deliverer to bring people out of sin and into the freedom of His Spirit.

That's why it's vitally important to understand that God doesn't want His people to be in bondage to anything at all. God purposefully made a distinction between His children and those who didn't serve Him (Exodus 11:7).

The final plague that came upon Egypt was God releasing the Death Angel who swept through the nation killing every firstborn male. Not only the humans, but the livestock and animals as well.

However, God gave His people an interesting instruction. He told them to sacrifice a lamb and smear its blood on the sides and top of the door frames of their homes.

When the Death Angel came through the land of Egypt, the blood on their doors served as a sign that God's covenant people lived there. The Death Angel was forced to pass over those houses and keep moving.

God said, "This plague of death will not touch you when I strike the land of Egypt" (See Exodus 12:12-13).

Even now, the Jewish people remember this day during the annual Passover celebration in obedience to God's Word (See Exodus 12:14). This miracle will never be forgotten. God wanted His people to remember His delivering power for the rest of eternity.

If the blood of a natural lamb kept the Death Angel from touching God's Old Testament people, how much more does the blood of the Eternal Lamb, Jesus Christ, keep the plagues of this world from touching us?

It's not just foolish for us to put our trust in humans who are imperfect, it's also dangerous.

In a time of elevated concern about healthcare and our personal well being, and as people grow increasingly fearful regarding the future, I have been prompted by the Holy Spirit to write this book as an encouragement to your faith.

My family has witnessed the miracle-working and protective power of God for four generations. We've seen miracle after miracle take place. There can be no doubt that God's power is not only real, it's still in operation today.

I want to show you throughout the Word of God how you can apply the power of the blood of Jesus to the door of your own home and walk in the protective power of covenant.

I've had people ask me, "Isn't it enough to just be a Christian?" If it were, there would be no sick Christians. Sadly, we see believers all over the world battling sickness and disease and falling prey to accidents. I'm not writing this to condemn anyone, because many times it isn't the fault of those believers. Unfortunately, many leaders either refuse to teach the fullness of God's Word, or they themselves are unaware of it.

God's Word is the basis for everything we will ever receive from the supernatural realm. It is the invisible force that sets you free (John 8:32). Consider this verse:

> *A man who wanders from the way of understanding (godly wisdom) Will remain in the assembly of the dead.*
>
> *Proverbs 21:16 AMP*

This means that people can be followers of God, but if they reject the power of His Word they will have the same results in their lives as those who don't follow Him.

Jesus is our Redeemer. Although sin, sickness, and poverty were our punishments for being separated from God, Jesus took our punishment to satisfy God's justice and instead gave us salvation, healing, and supernatural blessing.

That means our lives shouldn't look the same as someone who doesn't have a Redeemer. We should look redeemed.

I want to show you from Scripture the methods that God has given us to walk in supernatural protection no matter what is taking place around the world. I want you to remember several things as you read this book:

- It is not God's plan for you to live with or die of disease (Psalm 91:3).
- It is not God's plan for you to perish in a car or plane crash (Psalm 91:4).
- It is not God's plan for you to be destroyed by natural disasters (Psalm 91:6).
- It is not God's plan for you to be affected by terrorist attacks (Psalm 91:7).
- It is not God's plan for your life to be cut short at a young age (Psalm 91:16).

I pray that as you read this book, faith will rise in your heart. My desire is that you receive supernatural healing and deliverance from the Lord. I pray that every attack of the enemy against your life will be turned to a testimony in the mighty name of Jesus!

CHAPTER 2

YOU ARE UNCURSABLE

"But how can I curse those whom God has not cursed? How can I condemn those whom the Lord has not condemned? . . . God has blessed, and I cannot reverse it!"
—NUMBERS 23:8,20 NLT

When most people hear about curses or being cursed, they automatically define it as fiction.

Those people who have seen one too many movies about the supernatural discard unseen power as though it doesn't exist.

However, the Bible teaches that curses are real. In other nations where people strongly believe in supernatural power, demonic manifestations are seen and experienced on a regular basis.

Witch doctors and witches use demonic power to gain control of people and take advantage of them.

Many people who understand there are real unseen forces at work live in fear of being cursed.

I can't tell you how many people have approached

me with genuine concern asking me to pray that a generational curse would be broken off of their families.

If we're going to live in the protective power of covenant with God, we must understand how it pertains to curses and demonic forces that are at work in the earth. We shouldn't have to be afraid that evil people are sending curses against us.

I've seen Christians with dream catchers hanging from their rearview mirrors and good luck charms on their key chains. We don't have to become superstitious and work to ward off evil spirits, we just need to understand the Word of God.

THE CURSE OF THE LAW

The first curse I want to deal with is the curse of the Law which originated in the Old Testament when God gave instructions to His people as to how they should live.

Deuteronomy chapter 28 is a list of the blessings for obeying the Law of Moses and the curses for disobeying it.

The only problem with the Law of Moses is that it was an imperfect way to free people from sin and the curse of sin. By obeying the Law, sacrifices were made that covered the sins of Israel.

There was no way to remove Israel's sins; they could

only be covered by the blood of the sacrifice. Much like the method used by a child who stuffs everything under the bed rather than actually cleaning their room, the sins of Israel were "under the blood."

According to the Apostle Paul, the Law of Moses was given to God's people as a guardian to protect them until they could be made right with God through faith (Galatians 3:24).

That's where Jesus comes in.

Without Christ, there would be no way to be made right with God through faith. Two of the greatest Scriptures you'll ever read say:

> *But Christ has rescued us from the curse pronounced by the law. When he was hung on the cross, he took upon himself the curse for our wrongdoing. For it is written in the Scriptures, "Cursed is everyone who is hung on a tree." Through Christ Jesus, God has blessed the Gentiles with the same blessing he promised to Abraham, so that we who are believers might receive the promised Holy Spirit through faith.*
>
> **Galatians 3:13-14 NLT**

The curse of the Law of Moses was placed upon Christ's body when He was crucified. His death satisfied the justice of God. There is no longer any way for the curse of the Law to come upon us once we become believers. We are absolutely free.

If the devil is going to put a curse back on God's people, he would first have to travel into Heaven and wrestle it away from Jesus Who took it for us. That will never happen.

THE STOLEN LUNCH

The punishment for sin didn't belong to Jesus because He never sinned. It belonged to us, but Jesus took our place and accepted punishment on our behalf.

I once heard a parable illustrating this point. Decades ago, in the early 1900s, there was a one-room school house in the mountains of North Carolina that always had trouble keeping a teacher.

It seems there was a group of large, rough boys who took pride in running each new teacher off. The biggest and roughest boy in the group was named Jesse.

A new young teacher won the boys over, however, by letting them write the rules for the school which were very strictly enforced with a rod. For example, cheating would be punished with five strokes of the rod, and stealing with ten strokes, both to be given with the offender's coat off.

Everything went well until one day Jesse's lunch was stolen. A frail little boy in hand-me-down clothes that were too big for him admitted his guilt. The school rules demanded that he be whipped.

When the teacher called the little fellow up front, he came whimpering and begging to leave his coat on. The pupils insisted he obey the rules and take off his coat. When he did, a deathly silence settled over the room, for he had no shirt on and his emaciated body looked like skin stretched over bones. There were already bruises on his body, presumably from where a drunken father had beaten him.

The teacher gasped and dropped the rod. He knew he could never whip that little boy, but the rules were clear and couldn't be changed for one person.

With tears welling up in his eyes, Jesse stood up at his desk and walked to the front of the class. He stood between the frail boy and the teacher.

"I'll take it for him," he said. "After all, it was my lunch he stole." He shrugged off his coat.

At the third blow the rod broke, and the teacher threw it in the corner and said, "That's all, school dismissed!"

That little boy threw his arms around Jesse with tears streaming down his face.

"Thank you, Jesse. It would have killed me."

In the same way, Christ stood up for us and took a punishment that wasn't His to take. The punishment was so great that it would have killed us eternally, but thanks to the life and death of Jesus Christ, we are eternally set free from the judgment that awaited us.

GENERATIONAL CURSES

Once, during a revival my father was holding, a woman came to the altar for prayer after the service. She was very distraught.

"I want you to pray for my grandson," she said. "I'm afraid he's going to be an alcoholic."

"Why do you say that?" My father asked.

"It's a generational curse in our family," she replied. "My husband is an alcoholic, my son is an alcoholic, and now I think my grandson is going to be one too."

"All right, bring him here and I'll pray for him," my dad said. The woman walked out to the lobby and brought her grandson down the aisle to the altar.

Expecting to see her accompanied by a young man, my father was surprised to see she was bringing a little boy who was about five years old.

My dad looked at the little boy and said jokingly, "Have you been drinking too much root beer?"

The little boy wasn't becoming an alcoholic. His grandmother was just afraid that he would.

Living in fear gives the enemy access to your life. While faith is the currency that God uses to interact with His people, fear is the currency the enemy uses to interact with us.

That is what happened in the life of Job. He said that what he feared came upon him and what he dreaded came true (Job 3:25).

Is it possible for a believer to live under a curse that's passed down from generation to generation? One of the things that's important to note when dealing with this issue is that when we receive Christ as our Savior, we join a new family and become newly-created beings. Paul was very clear that old things have passed away and a new life has begun (2 Corinthians 5:17).

When speaking to the church in Rome, Paul explained it this way:

> *So you have not received a spirit that makes you fearful slaves. Instead, you received God's Spirit when HE ADOPTED YOU as his own children. Now we call him, "Abba, Father." (Emphasis added.)*
> *Romans 8:15 NLT*

The Apostle Paul drew an illustration from the Roman law of adoption. The modern laws of adoption are based on this very serious legal act before the Roman magistrates: a person opted to take a child into his family with the intent of treating the child as his own with all the privileges and responsibilities of that new family.

> **No matter what the story of previous generations has been, it does not have to be your story in Jesus' name.**

This is a very important law because the adopted child had all the rights of a legitimate son in his new family and at the same time he also lost all rights and responsibilities in his old family.

All of his old debts and obligations connected with the old family were abolished as if they never existed.

On the other hand, he now by right of the law stood as an heir to all of the inheritance of his new father. It was carried out in the presence of seven witnesses to make it official.

The Apostle Paul tells us that this is what God has done for us. This is now how He treats the believer in Jesus Christ. We had been members of old Adam's family with all of the effects of the curse of previous generations. We had been held responsible as members of that family.

But now, we have a new position before God with all

the legal rights and privileges (Romans 5:12-21).

Can you imagine Jesus Christ, the Son of the living God, walking around this earth cursed? Can you imagine our Savior not being able to make a marriage work or hold a job? Can you imagine Jesus not being able to live free from addictions or depression?

There is no curse strong enough to hold Christ in bondage, and through our supernatural adoption we stand in that same heavenly strength.

We should never again make statements like, "Cancer runs in my family. I hope I don't get it one day." No matter what the story of previous generations has been, it does not have to be your story in Jesus' name. You are redeemed and have supernatural privileges afforded to you by God.

SETTING THE WITCH DOCTOR ON FIRE

Dr. John G. Lake was a powerful man of God who experienced hundreds of thousands of unprecedented miracles throughout his life and ministry.

In 1914, he founded the Apostolic Church in Spokane, Washington, where his famous healing rooms attracted thousands from the United States and other countries.

In just five years, they recorded over 100,000 documented cases of healing. Sometime after, Spokane was called the healthiest city in the world.[1]

His ministry also extended to South Africa where he saw and wrote about many amazing signs and wonders that God performed.

While living in South Africa, he related the story of two native chiefs, living sixty miles apart, who had become extremely jealous of each other.

Once, while Dr. Lake was in the village of one of the chiefs, he overheard him discussing this difficulty with one of his men. It was decided by the chief that the next Sunday morning he was going to curse his rival and set him on fire.

Wanting to see this phenomenon, Dr. Lake saddled a horse and set out for the rival chief's village to arrive by Sunday morning.

When he arrived, the chief was out riding among his livestock. According to Dr. Lake, it was a normal Sunday exercise for the chiefs to go out and round up their herds and look over their flocks. He decided to ride along with the chief.

They hadn't ridden for more than an hour when he observed the chief becoming very hot. Within half an hour he was completely purple. Having some medical training, Dr. Lake was sure the man would have a stroke from high blood pressure.

After a while he began to complain of terrible pain.

Finally he became exhausted, got off his horse, and lay on the ground. Dr. Lake believed the man would die.

When it got to that point, Dr. Lake said, "It's time that we prayed."

He stepped over and laid hands on the chief and asked God to break the curse that was destroying him. God answered his prayer and shattered the demonic power instantly.[2]

THE CURSE OF MEN

Now that we've established that the curse of the Law and generational curses cannot touch you as a believer, the final curse I want to deal with is the curse of evil men. Make no mistake about it, there are those around the world who seek to operate in demonic power.

Just as in Dr. Lake's story I just related to you, there is a third type of curse that must be considered in this conversation.

I've had believers call me on the phone and ask me to pray for them because there were evil men and women in their region trying to place curses on them.

Should we be afraid or even cautious of the demonic power that's at work in the earth today?

I remember a story told by R.W. Schambach, who was a great evangelist and tent revivalist. His ministry was a wonderful example of God's miracle-working power.

A woman approached him for prayer during his tent crusade in Newark, New Jersey. She related to him that there were people in her neighborhood who didn't like her because she was a Christian. They were constantly trying to work magic against her.

Most recently, they had been performing voodoo rituals outside her house during the night. She would go out to get the paper in the morning only to find powder and a dead, bloody chicken on her doorstep.

"What should I do, Brother Schambach?" She asked.

"Girl, get out there and grab the chicken, dance in the powder and rejoice unto God!" He shouted back.

Brother Schambach knew that no one can curse God's children. In the Old Testament, a king tried to hire Balaam, a prophet of God, to curse God's people. Balaam asked the Lord about it and then told the king:

> *But how can I curse those whom God has not cursed? How can I condemn those whom the Lord has not condemned? . . . God has blessed, and I cannot reverse it!*
> *Numbers 23:8, 20 NLT*

No one can curse those on whom God has pronounced His blessing.

There is a promise that was given to us in God's Word. God spoke from Heaven and said:

> *I will bless those who bless you, And I will curse him who curses you;*
> *Genesis 12:3 NKJV*

It's much like the old phrase children have repeated for years: *I'm rubber, you're glue. Whatever you say bounces off of me and sticks to you.*

God, who cannot lie, said that He would make it His personal business to uphold your supernatural protection from demonic power. He was very clear about the fact that He would even curse evil men who attempted to bring a curse upon His children. When you take this into account, you realize it's in the devil's best interest not to mess with you.

The devil cannot destroy anyone he chooses. The Bible says regarding the limits of his power:

> *Your adversary the devil walks about like a roaring lion, seeking WHOM HE MAY DEVOUR. (Emphasis added.)*
> *1 Peter 5:8b NKJV*

Notice that he must seek out those whom he may devour. He cannot devour at will. So who can he devour? Those who do not know the new legal rights of belonging to the family of God.

If you're driving through London, England, on the right hand side of the road, you're going to be pulled over and ticketed and possibly cause an accident.

It doesn't matter how hard you try to explain to the officer that although people drive on the left hand side of the road in England, in America we drive on the right hand side of the road, the response you're likely to get is, "You're not in America anymore."

In the same way, when you become a Christian, you step into a new kingdom with new laws and rights. The devil no longer has any legal right to drive on your side of the road.

Sadly, some Christians are unaware of this principle and as a result cannot take advantage of their rights. The Word of God teaches that only the truth that you know can bring you into freedom (John 8:32).

The wonderful news is that we as believers are not under the curse of the law, we're not afflicted by any generational curse, and we cannot be cursed by evil men or women who have an antichrist agenda.

We are truly uncursable because of the power of the Holy Spirit Who lives within us.

#BLOODONTHEDOOR

THE DEVIL CAN'T DESTROY
A BELIEVER WHO IS
PROTECTED BY
THEIR PURPOSE.

CHAPTER 3

THE PROTECTIVE POWER OF DIVINE DIRECTION

*"They shall run like mighty men . . . and they shall not
break their ranks . . . they shall walk every one in his
path: and when they fall upon the sword, they shall not be
wounded."*
—JOEL 2:7-8 KJV

God is a God of plan and purpose. He has a specific purpose and calling for every one of His children. In the
same way that a manufacturer creates a product to accomplish a specific set of tasks, you have been created to
fulfill your divine purpose here on the earth.

My grandfather used to say, "You are not an accident,
you were created by divine design." You are unique and
your purpose has been tailor-made just for you.

Scripture compares our purpose to a race. However,
we don't get to choose which race we run throughout
our life. We must seek the face of God and discover our
individual purpose in the kingdom.

God has already laid our purpose out in the invisible
realm. We must pursue His presence to uncover it.

> *. . . let us run with endurance the race*
> *God has set before us.*
>
> *Hebrews 12:1 NLT*

Failing to discover God's specific plan and purpose for our lives can lead to a life of frustration. Furthermore, when we decide our own purpose, we are responsible for our own protection. When we follow God's plan and purpose, He said that He would be responsible to watch over us.

> *See, I am sending an angel before you*
> *to protect you on your journey and lead*
> *you safely to the place I have prepared*
> *for you. For my angel will go before you*
> *and bring you into the land of [your en-*
> *emies] so you may live there. And I will*
> *destroy them completely.*
>
> *Exodus 23:20, 23 NLT*

When God leads you in a specific direction, He takes supernatural measures of protection by dispatching angels to protect you along your journey.

With angelic assistance on your side, even in moments when you would otherwise be injured or killed, you can walk in supernatural protection.

THE NIGHT GOD BEAT UP A GANG

God had opened the door for my uncle, Evangelist Tiff Shuttlesworth, to hold an outdoor crusade just outside of Hyderabad, Telangana State, India.

This is a region of the world in desperate need of the gospel of Jesus Christ. Approximately 55% of the population is Hindu, 41% is Muslim, and only about 2.5% is Christian.[1]

Before the crusade began, the local ministers warned my uncle about a group of people who were very violent toward Christians and the gospel of Christ.

Other ministers I know have been instructed on such occasions not to preach against idol worship or false gods as it can anger the people of these nations where so many false gods are recognized and worshiped.

The crusade began and over 12,000 people gathered night after night under the humid air of the Indian sky to hear the wonderful gospel of Jesus.

As my uncle was preaching one night, out of the darkness came a high-pitched shriek followed by a man running onto the field and toward my uncle.

As the man tore across the field grasping a small club, my uncle could see he had violent intentions.

My uncle was preparing to defend himself but was prompted by the Holy Spirit to continue preaching.

When the man got about ten yards away from where my uncle was standing, he doubled over and fell to the ground as though he were dead.

My uncle described the incident later saying, "It looked like the man took a full 12-gauge shotgun blast to the stomach." The man had been struck by the power of God.

My uncle continued preaching until he was interrupted by another shriek. Moments later, a second figure appeared from the darkness. Just like the first man, he ran toward the platform with seemingly the same intentions.

When he got about ten yards from the platform, the same thing happened. He doubled over and fell on the ground, unmoving.

Although you would imagine these two examples of God's divine power would be enough to deter anyone else from disrupting the service, you must keep in mind the devil is a fool and full of pride . . . so he tried it one more time.

A shout followed by a third man running onto the field caught the attention of my uncle as he preached. God was no less accurate the third time than before. The third man also fell to the ground like he was dead.

The men remained unconscious on the field until people came, picked them up, and carried them away.

God was not going to allow demonic manifestations to hinder the preaching of the gospel of Christ that night. His protection and assistance were there because my uncle was operating by divine instruction.

I'm sure that if he had just decided that he was going to hold crusades in a hostile part of India and God had not instructed him to do so, the results would have been very different.

CAN'T SEEM TO CATCH A BREAK

There was a man in the Bible named Jonah. He received very specific instructions from God about what he was called to do. He was to travel to the city of Nineveh and announce God's judgment to the people because of their wickedness. He responded with disobedience:

> *Jonah got up and went in the opposite direction to get away from the Lord.*
> *Jonah 1:3 NLT*

It's never a good idea to do the exact opposite of what God tells you to do. Jonah took a boat going in the opposite direction.

As the ship sailed across the sea, a great storm arose that was so violent it threatened to break the ship apart.

The experienced sailors in the boat were all afraid for their lives.

The sailors encouraged Jonah to pray to his God and ask Him to spare their lives. However, there was no divine protection for Jonah as he was walking in complete disobedience to divine direction (Jonah 1:1-6).

It would have been impossible for Jesus to be destroyed by disaster, accident, or murder as He was always engaged in His divine purpose.

This story is very similar to one found in the New Testament. Jesus and his disciples got in a ship to cross the sea. Jesus said, "Let's cross to the other side of the lake," and they began their journey.

Because we know that Jesus only ever did what His Father in Heaven instructed Him, we know it was God's instruction that set them on this journey (John 5:19).

As in the story of Jonah, a great storm arose that would have destroyed Jesus' ship and killed every passenger. The outcome of this story, however, is much different. Jesus stood and rebuked the wind and the waves and everything became calm.

Why the difference? Unlike Jonah, Jesus was operating in obedience to divine direction.

THE INVINCIBLE JESUS

It would have been impossible for Jesus to be destroyed by disaster, accident, or murder, as He was always engaged in His divine purpose.

Time after time, Jesus faced impossible odds and always came out in perfect safety.

Once while He was teaching, He revealed Himself as the Messiah. The people in the synagogue were so enraged at His teaching that they mobbed Him and forced Him to the edge of the hill on which the town was built. They intended to push Him over the cliff, but He passed right through the crowd and went on His way (Luke 4:28-30).

One man versus a mob of angry men. How was He able to escape their plans to murder Him? He was operating under divine protection.

In another passage, Jesus was teaching along the same lines, and the men and women who were listening to Him became so angry that they picked up stones to stone Him to death for blasphemy (John 10:31-33).

Did they pick up stones to throw at Him? Yes. Why don't we have any record of even one stone being thrown, much less striking our Lord and Savior?

Divine protection.

In fact, Jesus used moments of crisis and turmoil to

draw a contrast to His magnificent power.

For example, after feeding 5,000 men with five loaves and two fish, He sent His disciples back to the other side of the lake while He went into the hills to pray.

As they began to row across the lake, the disciples were in trouble far away from land, for a strong wind had risen, and they were fighting heavy waves. About three o'clock in the morning Jesus came toward them, walking on the water (Matthew 14:22-25).

The disciples were in trouble and fighting for their lives. Jesus, on the other hand, was calmly walking on top of their trouble.

Why wasn't Jesus fighting for His life on the lake? He was walking in divine protection.

WHAT ABOUT THE DEATH OF JESUS?

Jesus wasn't completely invincible, I can hear some of you thinking. *They killed Him on the cross.*

Let's journey through the final moments of Jesus' life on the earth. It begins with the soldiers who came to arrest Him while He was with His disciples in the garden of Gethsemane.

Once again, Jesus was facing a crowd of armed men and soldiers. Apparently, it was overkill and a bit ridiculous because Jesus said, "Am I some dangerous revolutionary, that you come with swords and clubs to arrest me?" (Matthew 26:55). In the natural it looked like Jesus was no match for the men that had come to take Him.

Here is where we uncover the secret to His death.

Knowing all that would happen to Him, Jesus stepped forward and asked, "Who are you looking for?"

"Jesus the Nazarene," the soldiers said.

"I AM He," Jesus replied. When He said that, the power of God hit the soldiers and they all drew back and fell on the ground (John 18:4-6).

Interestingly, when Jesus said, "I AM," He wasn't merely identifying Himself. In the Old Testament when God sent Moses to deliver the Jews, Moses asked, "What should I tell them when they ask your name?"

> *God replied to Moses, "I AM WHO I AM.*
> *Say this to the people of Israel: I AM has*
> *sent me to you."*
> *Exodus 3:14 NLT*

Essentially, Jesus was revealing His power as the Son of God as He had done so many times before. The point was being made that He was not being taken by force; rather, He was willingly walking into His prophetic destiny of redemption.

In fact, Jesus' words were so powerful that He had

to stay silent through the majority of His trial and cru-
cifixion. This wasn't just to fulfill the prophecy that He
would be silent before His accusers (Isaiah 53:7), but it
ensured that the process would continue without delay.

Can you imagine the temptation of Jesus as He was
being tortured on the cross knowing that He could open
His mouth and call down a host of angels who would
deliver Him, but knowing that if He did the world
would be doomed? (Matthew 26:53-54).

Jesus was very clear that He was in control of his life
and no one could alter His destiny.

> *No one can take my life from me. I sacri-*
> *fice it voluntarily. For I have the author-*
> *ity to lay it down when I want to and*
> *also to take it up again. For this is what*
> *my Father has commanded.*
>
> *John 10:18 NLT*

No one could murder the Master. He walked in complete obedience to God's instruction and as a result lived
in divine protection throughout His entire life.

HOW DO I ACCESS DIVINE DIRECTION?

Undoubtedly, this is a subject that could fill another

book and there are some wonderful books that have already been written on divine direction. However, it would be pointless for me to share with you all of the benefits of obeying God's instruction but not show you how to attain it.

There are two major ways that we receive direction or instructions from Heaven: the Word of God and the voice of the Holy Spirit. David said:

> *Your word is a lamp to guide my feet and a light for my path.*
>
> **Psalm 119:105 NLT**

The Word will direct you and give you supernatural wisdom and direction for your personal life, ministry, and business. There are certain things in the Word of God that don't require the leading of the Spirit to obey.

For example, whether you're dealing with personal, ministry, or business finance, the Bible teaches a principle of having a reserve of resources at your disposal:

> *The wise have wealth and luxury, but fools spend whatever they get.*
>
> **Proverbs 21:20 NLT**

Many people roam the business aisles of their local

bookstores trying to find the secrets of promotion and success at their jobs. The Word of God gives us direction in one simple verse:

> *Observe people who are good at their work—skilled workers are always in demand and admired; they don't take a backseat to anyone.*
>
> *Proverbs 22:29 The Message*

I knew a girl who begged her father to co-sign on a loan so that her deadbeat boyfriend could buy a car. He relented and the boyfriend was able to buy the car.

Months later, the boyfriend was nowhere to be found and the bank was calling the father to make the payments on a car that shouldn't have been his responsibility. He could very easily have been protected from this situation if he had read just one verse:

> *Don't agree to guarantee another person's debt or put up security for someone else.*
>
> *Proverbs 22:26 NLT*

Simply obeying the Word of God will save you from issues that you didn't even know were coming. The

Scriptures are divine wisdom direct from the mouth of God. He inspired men to write His inerrant Word so that we may hold divine wisdom in our hands (Proverbs 2:6).

Obeying the Word of God is obedience to Heaven's unfailing wisdom. There are scriptural benefits to attaining the wisdom of God:

> *Don't turn your back on wisdom, for she will protect you. Love her, and she will guard you.*
>
> *Proverbs 4:6 NLT*

God's Word has supernatural power to protect and guard you when it is obeyed.

Divine direction is essential for every step we take in life. When we receive and obey it, we can be assured that we will be successful in every endeavor. That is why God spoke to Joshua and said:

> *Study this Book of Instruction continually. Meditate on it day and night so you will be sure to obey everything written in it. Only then will you prosper and succeed in all you do.*
>
> *Joshua 1:8 NLT*

It's dangerous to only crack your Bible open on Sunday morning when your pastor begins his sermon. Dig into the vast treasury of supernatural wisdom and watch as it brings protection to your life and family.

The second way we receive divine direction from God is from the voice of the Holy Spirit which is accessed through prayer.

Prayer is such an important aspect of living in the protective power of our covenant relationship with God. I will deal with the amazing benefits attached to the power of prayer in the next chapter.

GOD WILL SPEAK EARLY SO THAT YOUR PROTECTION IS NEVER LATE.

CHAPTER 4

THE PROTECTIVE POWER OF PRAYER

"Ask me and I will tell you remarkable secrets you do not know about things to come."
—JEREMIAH 33:3 NLT

Prayer plays a vital role in our divine protection. It is our communication with God that allows us to hear His voice.

When He speaks to us, He has the ability to give us instruction. When that instruction is obeyed, we can rest in knowing that His plans always succeed. Failure is not an option when obeying the voice of the Lord. As long as we're operating by divine direction we cannot fail (Isaiah 55:11).

The reason we can be sure of this is because God knows what will happen in the future.

Did you know that at the time it was written, the Bible was over 33% prophecy? One-third of God's Word was written regarding things that would happen in the future. Approximately 80% of the predictions have already come to pass with complete and total accuracy.

I once heard a man say, "If you're going to accurately predict the future, one of two things has to be true. Either you built a time machine, traveled into the future, came back and told everyone what was going to happen, or you must be God."

God knows the end from the beginning. Consider this statement He made through the prophet Isaiah:

> *Only I can tell you the future before it even happens. Everything I plan will come to pass, for I do whatever I wish.*
> *Isaiah 46:10 NLT*

That's why when God speaks to us, it's very important that we obey His voice. No matter how long we have served the Lord as believers, we will never outgrow the need for His instructions.

GOD WILL WARN YOU AHEAD OF TIME

In his book, *Following God's Plan for Your Life*, Kenneth Hagin relates a story of how God gave him divine instructions that protected him during a time of economic crisis in America.

After twenty-six years of full-time ministry, God woke him up one day just before 6:00 a.m. and he sat straight up in bed. The Lord said to him,

"An economic crunch is coming to the nation. Get ready for it. If you'll do what I tell you to do, you'll feel the effects of the crunch, but it won't affect you as it does other people."

He wrote down exactly what the Lord instructed him to do. The Lord said, "Number one, stop operating in outreaches I never told you to get involved with in the first place. Number two, trim *Failure is not an option when obeying the voice of the Lord. As long as we're operating by divine direction we cannot fail.* your payroll by laying off this many people from your staff," (and he told Brother Hagin exactly how many people to lay off). "Number three, cut back on expenses. Operate the ministry on 90 percent of your incoming cash flow and save the other 10 percent."

He immediately set about obeying the Lord's instructions. He laid off the employees that the Lord specified and got out of the various outreaches the Lord never told him to begin.

He testified that the financial downturn came just as God said it would, but his ministry never felt the effects of it because of the instructions he obeyed ahead of time.[1]

There is an aspect of God's character that allows us to be constantly led into profitable situations. He spoke through the prophet Isaiah and said:

> *Thus says the Lord, your Redeemer, the Holy One of Israel: "I am the Lord your God, who teaches you to profit, who leads you in the way you should go.*
> *Isaiah 48:17 ESV*

God wants to speak to you ahead of time because He doesn't want to see His children in distress or destruction. His love for us is so great that He reveals the future to us so that we can be prepared for what's coming.

PT CRASHER

In between my first and second year of Bible school I bought a Chrysler PT Cruiser. I laugh looking back at how I thought that was the most beautiful vehicle I had ever seen. In retrospect, it looked like something Dick Tracy would have driven. (Sorry to every reader who owns a PT Cruiser.)

When I returned to college after the summer, I got a job working the third shift at a call center. I began each night at 11:00 p.m., finished at 8:00 a.m., and had to be in class by 8:30 a.m.

One week, instead of resting my body properly while on this schedule, I foolishly decided to stay up all night and the next day. After having been awake for twenty-seven hours, I was driving to work a nine-hour shift.

As I was driving down 71st street in Broken Arrow, Oklahoma, I fell dead asleep at the wheel.

Still holding the steering wheel, I pulled my car through two lanes of oncoming traffic. Not one car hit me. I entered the parking lot of a restaurant but never hit one car or pedestrian. My car went over the cement blocks

God wants to speak to you ahead of time because He doesn't want to see His children in distress or destruction.

at the end of the parking spaces and I woke up driving through a field of grass. My car came to a stop in the middle of a warehouse parking lot.

I didn't even have a seat belt on. I got out of the car and realized that although my car was severely damaged, there was not one scratch or bruise on my body.

I called my father to let him know what happened, and he had his own story to tell me.

Earlier that day, while he was going about his usual business, the Lord showed my father a vision of me getting into a car accident.

At that moment he stopped what he was doing and began to pray for me to be divinely protected until he felt peace in his spirit.

I'm sure his prayers saved my life that day. Prayer is a divine avenue into the protective power of God. That's why we should be eternally grateful for the Holy Spirit Who teaches us to pray and intercedes for us even when we don't know what to pray (Romans 8:26).

COMFORTER. GUIDE. TEACHER.

Aside from Jesus, the Holy Spirit is the greatest gift that God ever delivered to the earth.

The disciples wanted Jesus to stay on the earth and set up His kingdom. Jesus explained to them that it wasn't just important that He had come, but it was equally important that He leave so that He could send the Holy Spirit to them (John 16:5-7).

> *When the Spirit of truth comes, he will guide you into all truth. He will not speak on his own but will tell you what he has heard. He will tell you about the future.*
>
> *John 16:13 NLT*

The Holy Spirit was sent to us as our teacher and guide. Prayer is our God-given avenue to communicate with the Holy Spirit. What good does it do knowing we have a God Who knows all things, but never asking Him to reveal them to us?

There is a huge difference between benefiting from someone's actions and knowing their methods. Knowing their methods is much more beneficial because it ensures that you can activate their process for yourself.

You may have heard a phrase that has been modified and popularized from an old novel, *Mrs. Dymond*, which says, "Give a man a fish and you feed him for a day; teach a man to fish and you feed him for a lifetime."

We're not to live our lives hoping that God will bless us with the proverbial fish, we're to petition Him for an instruction. He will show us the future so that we may catch our own fish, so to speak.

We see the distinction between these two types of people in the Old Testament:

> *He made known his ways to Moses, his*
> *acts to the people of Israel.*
> *Psalm 103:7 ESV*

The people of Israel merely waited on the miracles of

God. They were benefiting from His actions. Moses, on the other hand, had a behind-the-scenes look into the ways and methods of God.

That's what an atmosphere of prayer will cultivate in your personal life. You don't have to be a super-Christian to hear the voice of the Lord, you just have to obey God's command to call on Him so that He may answer you (Jeremiah 33:3).

The power of protection that surrounds our lives is generated by embarking only on what God leads you to do. Although this is taught throughout the Word of God, the clearest picture of this principle may be found in Psalm 127:

> *Unless the Lord builds a house, the work of the builders is wasted. Unless the Lord protects a city, guarding it with sentries will do no good.*
>
> *Psalm 127:1 NLT*

We as believers can know what we have been designed by God to do and don't have to wander through life searching for purpose.

Why should a Christian college student go to a university, erratically change majors two or three times, rack up more student loan debt, and battle frustration, all because they're unsure of their calling?

Doesn't God have a plan for his or her life? Absolutely. Many times we deal with frustrations that we shouldn't have to because we don't seek guidance from the Holy Spirit.

If you're single, you don't have to get together with the first person that shows interest in you. How many times do people get into trouble because they form unhealthy (sometimes harmful) relationships?

It's hard for me to believe that God has such specific plans for the lives of His children, but takes no interest in who they marry. God has someone for you.

We as believers can know what we have been designed by God to do and don't have to wander through life searching for purpose.

When I first met my wife, Carolyn, and began to get to know her, I liked her immediately. I didn't have to grow to like her. In fact, the first time I ever saw her walk into church, I instantly wanted to find out who she was.

After a few months had passed and we'd spent time together, I was ready to move forward, but I didn't want to take a step in the wrong direction if it wasn't what the Lord wanted for my life. There are many wonderful people in the world, but they're not all for you.

So in March of 2005, I began to fast and pray for three

days. From Good Friday until Easter Sunday night I prayed. That might not seem to you like a long time for such an important decision, but I figured if God could raise Jesus from the dead in three days, it wouldn't take longer than that to reveal who my wife should be.

Easter Sunday night I got the green light from the Holy Spirit. I sent a quick text to my mom telling her that she could stop praying for a wife for me, and then I called Carolyn to see when we could go out.

When I met her that night on our first official date, I told her I loved her and that I believed she was my wife. Basically, in a one-hour period I said all the things that would make a woman think I was crazy and run from me. But Carolyn didn't run. She didn't think I was crazy either. She knew we were supposed to be together.

Confirmation is a wonderful thing. God is interested even in your relationships.

PRAYER THAT BRINGS PROTECTION

I've often said while preaching, "If you love someone, you're not trying to see when you can get away from them, you're trying to spend even more time with them."

When Carolyn and I were engaged, I would leave work as soon as I was finished and without any delay, I would drive straight to wherever she was. I wanted to spend the most time with her that I could.

When she was talking to me, I wasn't thinking, *I wish she would shut up so I can get out of here. I'd like to hit a drive-thru before they all close.*

It's funny how when you're in love with someone you just want to hear whatever they have to say. It's the only time you'll hear men say things like, "Eyebrow threading? Sounds amazing! Tell me all about it."

You don't care. You're just happy to be with them, talking to them, and spending time together.

That's why if we say we love God, we shouldn't find it laborious to spend time in prayer. We should look forward to it and find it exciting, knowing that God is going to reveal important details regarding our future.

Although many Christians have asked me how much time they should spend in prayer, I can't answer that question. I'm not the Holy Spirit.

I can, however, give you some guidelines that I feel are wise to take into account when considering your prayer life.

1. No leftovers. Imagine how your husband or wife would feel if after a long day of work you came home to spend time with your family, but instead of engaging with them meaningfully, you plopped down on the couch and zoned out while they talked to you. You're not giving them your best. In the same way, prayer should not be left until you have some free time left over after all of the "important" things are done.

Prayer should be given priority in your life. There is nothing that carries such an importance as your personal prayer life. The Bible records that many times Jesus would get up before dawn to go out in the wilderness to pray. He made it the first thing He did (Mark 1:35).

2. *Spend quality time.* In my book, *Praise. Laugh. Repeat.*, I dealt with the recent statistic that Christians in America only pray for an average of five minutes each day.[2]

Nothing of value is given five minutes each day. This book took six to eight hours of writing each day, not to mention the time in editing and proofreading.

Body builders spend hours each day at the gym sculpting and perfecting their physiques. Doctors spend years developing their understanding of the human body and its functions. Any meaningful relationship requires an investment of quality time.

Dr. Yonggi Cho, who pastors the largest congregation in the world (over one million), wrote that he will not even stand in the pulpit to preach in nations where he can sense a spiritual resistance until he has prayed between four and six hours.[3]

It seems the early church spent at least an hour each

day in prayer. Acts chapter 3 tells us that Peter and John were going to the temple during the "hour of prayer."

Jesus encouraged His disciples along these lines when He said, "Couldn't you watch with me even one hour?" (Matthew 26:40).

I believe that an hour of prayer each day is a good starting point for every believer. Some would argue that they're too busy and don't have that extra time. The truth is, we all find time to do the things we want to do.

We must have a hunger and desire for the presence of God in our lives above and beyond anything else.

3. Base your prayers on God's Word. God is only responsible to honor His Word. In fact, He has backed His Word with the authority of His name (Psalm 138:2).

Many Christians that I've talked to have told me, "I try to pray, but after about three or four minutes I run out of things to say."

I'm so happy I found a method to overcome this type of stagnant prayer. Two mighty men of God in Nigeria, Dr. Enoch Adeboye and Bishop David Oyedepo, have taught their churches to pray using prayer points.

These are lists of prayers based upon the Word of God. For example, they may pray based on Psalm 68:1-2 and ask God to arise and scatter every enemy of the Christian church by His mighty power. They will pray that anything that would hold back the gospel from being preached throughout the earth would be driven away like the wind would drive away smoke. These prayer points are merely guidelines to keep your prayers based upon Scripture, not to rule out Spirit-led prayer or become a religious ritual.

4. *Couple your prayer with fasting.* This adds a certain boost to your prayer life. There are many who do not understand the action of fasting. They feel like it's an ancient religious ritual that's not relevant today. As I did with prayer, I want to devote the next chapter to the power of fasting.

I want to encourage you to get started now at whatever level you may find yourself. Set time aside to pray and seek the face of God and He will undoubtedly reward you.

CHAPTER 5

THE PROTECTIVE POWER OF FASTING

"His disciples asked Him privately, 'Why could we not cast it out?' So He said to them, 'This kind can come out by nothing but prayer and fasting.'"
—MARK 9:28-29 NKJV

Fasting seems to be one of the most controversial topics in the body of Christ today. Some might ask if it's necessary for the New Testament believer. It might appear to be a habit formed out of a "works-based mentality."

However, we need to understand that fasting is not only a biblical principle, it's an expectation of Jesus for the New Testament believer. When asked about His disciples' fasting habits He said:

> *Do wedding guests mourn while celebrating with the groom? Of course not. But someday the groom will be taken away from them, and then they will fast.*
> *Matthew 9:15 NLT*

He was saying that when He returned to Heaven, His followers would continue on in fasting and prayer as they did in previous generations.

In His Sermon on the Mount, Jesus took time to teach about prayer and fasting combined together. We can see that He didn't view fasting as optional, nor did He look at it as a once-in-a-lifetime event.

He said plainly, "*When* you fast," as He expected His followers to be engaged in this habit throughout their lives. He instructed His disciples not to announce it, but to make it a private action of obedience that God would then reward openly (Matthew 6:16-18).

One misconception about fasting is that its only purpose is to weaken your flesh, making you more sensitive to the Spirit of God. While that is one benefit, the Bible shows us that fasting coupled with prayer is also a spiritual transaction that unlocks supernatural power on your behalf.

THE BENEFITS OF FASTING

God spoke through the prophet Isaiah to the people of Israel. He gave them instructions about fasting and prayer and revealed the benefits that would result from their obedience.

As we take a closer look at what God said in Isaiah

chapter 58, we'll see that there are five distinct blessings that are released when we engage His presence in fasting and prayer. Let's look at the Scriptures describing God's chosen fast and then examine the benefits.

> *Is this not the fast that I have chosen: To loose the bonds of wickedness, To undo the heavy burdens, To let the oppressed go free, And that you break every yoke? Then your light shall break forth like the morning, Your healing shall spring forth speedily, And your righteousness shall go before you; The glory of the Lord shall be your rear guard. Then you shall call, and the Lord will answer.*
>
> *Isaiah 58:6, 8, 9 NKJV*

1. Your light shall break forth like the morning. When the Bible speaks of light, it is speaking of revelation knowledge. Divine understanding of God's Word sets us on another level in the supernatural realm.

David said that God's Word became a lamp for his feet and a light unto his path (Psalm 119:105). As I previously mentioned, your level of understanding of God's Word determines the level of freedom you will experience in your life (John 8:32). The path of your life becomes illuminated by your revelation and understanding of Scripture.

I remember the first time I ever experienced this explosion of revelation in my life. I was fasting and praying and had set aside time to hear from God and read His Word. I grabbed my notebook and pen and sat down in my office. I began by praying and thanking God that He was opening the eyes of my understanding as I read.

Redemption is not a package of promises; it is a collection of covenant terms.

I opened my Bible expecting to read John chapter 1 through chapter 9 in the time that I had allotted for myself to study.

As I read through John chapter 1, God began to release revelation that I never had before. I furiously scribbled notes in my journal as God showed me things in the first chapter of John's Gospel. When I finally looked down at my watch as I prepared to move on to chapter 2, I was surprised to find that I had spent my entire allotted time in just one chapter.

I had made almost four pages of notes on just one chapter of the Bible. What happened? *My light broke forth like the morning.*

The first benefit of fasting and prayer that is promised by God is that you will gain an supernatural understanding of His Word. This one aspect of fasting and prayer opens a whole new world of possibilities to you as a follower of Christ.

2. *Your healing shall spring forth speedily.* The second thing clearly promised as a benefit of fasting and prayer is that divine healing will quickly manifest in your body.

Wait a minute, I can hear some of you thinking. *Healing was purchased for us by the blood of Jesus on the cross. Why should we have to do anything else to receive it?*

This is a common question that many believers have. While the combination of fasting and prayer is not the only way that believers may receive healing from God, it is one avenue given to us to activate that blessing.

One thing we must understand about redemption is that it is not a package of promises; rather, it is a collection of covenant terms.

More simply, none of the blessings we receive from God come to us automatically. Each one must be received and appropriated by faith.

If God's blessings were automatic, then Jesus' death alone would have set the world right with God. There would be no more sinners left on the earth and we could all go directly to Heaven.

However, Jesus' death was only God's half of the covenant transaction. Now, if we want to receive salvation, we also have a part to play.

The Bible says that we must confess that Jesus is Lord and believe in our hearts that God raised Him from the dead. That is our response to God that completes the transaction of salvation (Romans 10:9).

Without that action of faith, we are not entitled to salvation. In the same way, God gave us a covenant of financial blessing in redemption (2 Corinthians 8:9). Does that mean that all Christians are wealthy and have no needs? Absolutely not.

Until our half of the covenant is activated, we have no right to obtain financial blessing (Luke 6:38).

You can readily see that any blessings God has provided for His children must be obtained forcefully by faith. In fact, the Bible says:

> *And from the days of John the Baptist until now the kingdom of heaven suffers violence, and the violent take it by force.*
> *Matthew 11:12 NKJV*

Our healing, like any other aspect of the covenant, must be obtained and activated by forceful faith that takes action.

God created our bodies and knows more about them than any doctor or specialist on the earth.

Though fasting is an action of faith and obedience,

God also understands the need for our bodies to be cleansed from the harmful toxins that pass through it on a regular basis.

Tests have proven that the average American consumes and assimilates four pounds of chemical preservatives, coloring, stabilizers, flavorings, and other additives each year. These build up in our bodies and cause illness and disease. Periodic fasts are necessary to flush out the poisons. Fasting gives your body time to heal itself. It relieves tension and gives your digestive system a rest. Fasting lowers your blood pressure and can lower your cholesterol.[1]

Dr. Oda H. F. Birchinger, who supervised more than 70,000 fasts, stated, "Fasting is a royal road to healing, for anyone who agrees to take it, for recovery and regeneration of the body, mind, and spirit." He continued, "Fasting can heal and help rheumatism in the joints and muscles, diseases of the heart, circulation, blood vessels, stress-related exhaustion, skin diseases — including pimples and complexion problems, irregular menstrual cycles and hot flashes, disease of respiratory organs, allergies such as hay fever and other eye diseases."[2]

In his book *Toxic Relief*, Dr. Don Colbert writes about the body's need to rid itself of toxins that cause illness, disease, fatigue, and many other issues.

He writes, "Fasting does not only prevent sickness.

If done correctly, fasting holds amazing healing benefits to those of us who suffer illness and disease. From colds and flu to heart disease, fasting is a mighty key to healing the body."[3]

Jentezen Franklin, who has authored multiple books, articles, and many sermons on the subject of fasting concludes, "Fasting slows your aging process. Moses fasted often, including two forty-day fasts, and the Bible says in Deuteronomy 34:7, 'Moses was one hundred and twenty years old when he died. His eyes were not dim nor his natural vigor diminished.'"[4]

Without a doubt, God knew fasting had natural benefits as well as spiritual ones when He commanded His children to engage in it.

Fasting and prayer allow you to take action and obtain from God what belongs to you through your covenant with Jesus.

3. *Your righteousness shall go before you.* Native Americans have played an integral role in U.S. military conflicts since America's beginning.

Colonists recruited Native American allies during such instances as the Pequot War, the Revolutionary War, and the War of 1812.

Native Americans also fought on both sides during the American Civil War, as well as military missions abroad. One of the most notable contributions made by Native Americans was by the Code Talkers who served in World War II.[5]

Even during smaller conflicts like the Nez Percé Campaign of 1877, the American Indian scouts were a fast-moving, aggressive, and knowledgeable asset to the U.S. Army. They often proved to be immune to Army notions of discipline and demeanor, but they proved expert in traversing the vast distances of the American West and providing intelligence—and often a shock force—to the soldiers who sought hostile tribes.

One chief of scouts, Stanton G. Fisher, emphasized the importance of Native American Scouts by saying of the soldiers, "Uncle Sam's boys are too slow for this business."[6]

We need to activate supernatural assistance from the Lord to successfully navigate our purpose.

The job of the scouts was to move ahead of the Army and gather intelligence about what was ahead, and if possible, clear the way for the forces behind them.

In the same way that Fisher realized the U.S. military needed the assistance of the Native American scouts because they were ill-equipped to handle the conditions they faced, we need supernatural assistance to successfully navigate our purposes.

This benefit is supernaturally afforded to us through

fasting and prayer. The prophet Jeremiah declared that the Lord is our righteousness (Jeremiah 23:6). This means that the Lord will go ahead of us and prepare the way, warn us of things to come, and fight on our behalf.

A perfect picture of this happening is when the Lord spoke to King Cyrus through the prophet Isaiah. He assured him of success when He said:

> *I will go before you, Cyrus, and level the mountains. I will smash down gates of bronze and cut through bars of iron. And I will give you treasures hidden in the darkness — secret riches.*
>
> *Isaiah 45:2-3 NLT*

Every hindrance that stands in your way will be leveled by the power of God. One translation of this passage says that God will "make the crooked places straight." This has special significance because when your path is crooked, it slows your momentum.

Think about it. Anytime there is a race that measures how fast someone or something is, many times it's conducted in a straight line. Whether it's the 100-yard dash or a car company calculating how quickly their new vehicle accelerates from zero to sixty miles per hour, it's done on a straight path.

When you have to make turns or avoid obstacles, you always have to slow down and lose momentum. I'm always frustrated watching the skiing event in the Olympics where participants have to ski way out around the flags as they come down the mountain. It takes too long. Of course, this is coming from the guy who likes to go to the very top of the steepest hill, tuck my poles under my arms and fly down the mountain as fast as I can.

God wants you to be able to run your Christian race with power and momentum. It's the enemy who wants to slow you down and put obstacles in your path.

When the Lord goes before you, He won't just remove hindrances from your path, He will connect you with the people that He has called you to help and those who will help you.

THE FAST THAT BROUGHT COLONEL SANDERS TO JESUS

Pastor Waymon Rodgers, who founded the 9,000-member Evangel World Prayer Center in Louisville, Kentucky, was a man of prayer and fasting.

In the mid-1970s he was fasting, praying, and asking God to bring revival to their church. God answered his prayer and a seventeen-week revival broke out.

During the revival, someone had the courage to walk up to Kentucky Fried Chicken founder Colonel Harland

Sanders on the street, and with just a friendly word, invited him to attend special evangelistic services and to hear good singing. Pastor Rodgers remembers how it happened:

> I saw him come in. You couldn't miss him in a crowd, with his white suit and his identifying white beard and full head of hair. I knew God was going to do something special that night. I felt it immediately. Our people had been praying.
>
> As our evangelist moved into the service, I left the platform and sat with the Colonel on the front pew. The invitation began. He raised his hand for prayer. There were tears. I said, "Colonel, let's get down on our knees and talk to God."
>
> "I don't know what to say," he replied.
>
> "Let's start with the sinner's prayer," I suggested.
>
> "God be merciful to me, a sinner," the Colonel said.' [I] will always remember how the Colonel's problem tumbled out. A stain, stubborn and shameful, had fastened itself to this proud, successful man's life. He wanted to be free from cursing, which festered his ordinary conversation. He was never free from it. It made him feel as rotten as liquor does a drunkard. It was the

one bad thing he had learned to do during his years of railroading. It marked him.

He had tried in vain to break the habit. This was proof enough that he was not saved, no matter how often he attended church.

Suddenly the Colonel lifted his head. He looked at me and told me that it was the first time he had ever experienced the presence of Christ within his heart. A moment or two later, I suggested that we talk to God together about his problem of cursing.

He said, "Pastor Rodgers, we don't need to do that. Christ has done that for me already."[7]

Not long after Colonel Sanders' conversion, he gave one million dollars to the church. This also was an answer to Pastor Rodgers' fasting and prayer, and it was a great testimony as God had increased the church so steadily that they had to build a larger building.

Fasting and prayer cause the power of God to go before you and prepare the way for your glorious destiny.

4. *The glory of the Lord shall be your rear guard.* I've heard it said that the elements of the Armor of God, which are described in detail in Ephesians chapter 6, are designed to only cover the front of the believer. The reasoning behind this statement is that God never expects His soldiers to retreat from their enemy.

While this point might elicit shouting and dancing during a sermon on the victorious church, I've always found the argument a bit thin.

I find it hard to believe that God would protect us from the front, but fail to protect us from behind.

This verse clearly shows us that through fasting and prayer, the glory of God becomes our rear guard. He protects us from behind no matter what our enemy may have planned to destroy us.

It's a wonderful thing to know that God's got your back. He never wants to see us fail, but many times we're so busy with the details of life that we don't hear His voice, or we don't petition Him by faith to receive secrets about the future (Jeremiah 33:3).

Remember, everything we receive from God must be received by faith. If actions of faith are not present, there is nothing to motivate God to move on our behalf.

Prayer and fasting are faith actions that motivate God to reveal hidden things regarding our future. According to the book of James, one of the main reasons we don't have what God has prepared for us is because we fail to ask Him for it (James 4:3).

The Bible is very clear:

No weapon turned against you will succeed. You will silence every voice raised up to accuse you. These benefits are enjoyed by the servants of the Lord; their vindication will come from me. I, the Lord, have spoken!

Isaiah 54:17 NLT

When we serve the Lord, we enjoy these benefits. You don't have to be afraid of the sneak attack your enemy is planning against you. There are no "terrors of the night" that can overtake you (Psalm 91:5). Fasting and prayer empower you to be guarded on every side by the glory of the most high God.

5. Then shall you call, and the Lord will answer. One of the wonderful benefits of prayer coupled with fasting that we see throughout the Word of God is that it expedites the answers to our prayers.

While we as New Testament believers may not need to fast to have our prayers answered, there is no question that fasting is a powerful supplement to our prayers.

Sadly, many Christians don't pray as often or as diligently as God would like. This is a major roadblock that causes them to be stuck at a certain point in their purpose for an extended period of time, allowing stagnation to set in.

One thing fasting definitely accomplishes is it keeps us in the mindset and atmosphere of prayer throughout our day. It weakens the flesh, giving way to the desires of the spirit.

It's important to understand that God doesn't reward every believer. He rewards those who diligently seek His face (Hebrews 11:6).

Fasting and prayer are undeniable access points into the presence of God and proof that you are seeking Him diligently. God spoke to the prophet Jeremiah and said:

> *And you will seek Me and find Me, when you search for Me with all your heart. I will be found by you, says the Lord.*
> *Jeremiah 29:13-14 NKJV*

In his definitive book on fasting, *God's Chosen Fast*, Arthur Wallis writes, "When a man is willing to set aside the legitimate appetites of the body to concentrate on the work of praying, he is demonstrating that he means business, that he is seeking with all his heart, and will not let God go unless He answers."[8]

I'll never forget when fasting and prayer opened the door to the supernatural for our ministry. I was praying one day and asked God to let us see more miracles in the upcoming year than we had ever seen before.

God's reply shocked me. "You've gone as far as you can go at your current level of prayer, " He said. It felt like a slap in the face, but rather than getting mad, I entered into a time of extended prayer and fasting.

Although I had begun the year with a twenty-one-day fast, I felt prompted by the Spirit of God to repeat this process in the fall of that year.

During those twenty-one days, I focused my prayers asking God to use me to bring deliverance and healing to His people. During the final days of that fast, I was holding a meeting in Canada.

A woman attended one night who had never been to church in her life. At the end of the service she accepted Jesus as her Savior. When she heard we would be praying for healing, she brought her six-year-old son, Timothy, forward to receive prayer.

"He's been totally blind in one eye for five years," she told me. "I believe if you'll pray for him, God will open his eye." I felt a supernatural compassion wash over me that I had never felt. I was reminded of the Scripture:

> *So Jesus had compassion and touched their eyes. And immediately their eyes received sight . . .*
> *Matthew 20:34 NKJV*

I reached down and hugged the little boy. Laying my hands on his eye, I prayed and asked God to open it by His power. When I removed my hand, the little boy said, "I can see you!"

His mother collapsed to the ground and began to cry as God gave him back his sight.

Since that day, we have witnessed many mighty miracles by the power of the Holy Spirit. Fasting and prayer continue to lead us into supernatural results every year.

Jesus explained to His disciples that there are different levels of supernatural opposition. When they failed to conquer a case of demonic possession, they were confused at their lack of results. Jesus explained that fasting and prayer are necessary to prevail against certain types of spiritual adversary (Mark 9:17-29).

Without a doubt, fasting and prayer allow you to walk in the protective power of God. We've seen that it is the expectation of Jesus for His followers throughout their lives. More than just a religious discipline, the combination of fasting and prayer is a supernatural transaction that unlocks divine intervention.

No one can tell you how long to fast and pray. We must be led by the Spirit of God.

I want to encourage you to begin fasting and praying throughout the year. Set time aside to seek the face of God. He is interested in leading you in every aspect of life. We need to hear His voice and obtain His direction like never before.

Answers are waiting for you in the presence of God. Hear His voice today and activate the protective power of covenant in your life and family.

CHAPTER 6

THE PROTECTIVE POWER OF PRAISE

"At the very moment they began to sing and give praise, the Lord caused the armies of Ammon, Moab, and Mount Seir to start fighting among themselves."
—2 CHRONICLES 20:22 NLT

Praise is a subject that is often misunderstood. If you were to ask most Christians what praise is, they might tell you that it's the fast songs sung before the slow ones at church. But praise is more than just singing, dancing, or playing an instrument in worship.

Praise is a spiritual transaction that yields supernatural results. Throughout the Word of God we see story after story that describes God's intervention because of the praise that His children offered up to Him. Something takes place when you praise God:

> *Yet you are holy, enthroned on the praises of Israel.*
>
> *Psalm 22:3 NLT*

This verse shows us very clearly that God is actively involved in the praises of His people. In fact, the word translated "enthroned" is the Hebrew word *yashab*.

According to Strong's Concordance, it could be more fully translated "to make habitation."

We begin to see that when we praise God, He dwells amidst our praises. He becomes actively involved when we praise Him.

Praise is a spiritual transaction that provokes God to supernatural action. Something has to change when we praise God. The British evangelist Smith Wigglesworth once said, "If God doesn't move me, I'll move God."

Praise is a spiritual transaction that provokes God to supernatural action.

Although that may sound arrogant to some, Wigglesworth understood that faith would cause God to move on his behalf. Praise is an outward demonstration of inward faith. When you begin to give thanks and praise to God for something He hasn't even done in your life yet, you are essentially praising Him on credit, knowing that He is able to accomplish it and it's already done.

There is never a question about whether God is able to accomplish what He said He would do. The question is whether we are willing to pursue and provoke Him to action (Ephesians 3:20).

BLIND WITH PERFECT VISION

Jesus and His disciples were on a journey to Jerusalem when they found themselves passing through the city of Jericho.

A blind beggar named Bartimaeus, who was the son of Timaeus, was sitting beside the road. I've always found it interesting that Mark, the writer of the Gospel, took great care to give us the name of Bartimaeus' father.

When the Bible takes the time to list a person's lineage, it's to give us a certainty about their distinction and importance. In fact, the Bible lists Jesus' lineage for forty-two generations for that very purpose (Matthew 1:1-17).

It encourages me to know that God is showing us here that even though this man is a blind beggar, he is still important.

No matter what attack the enemy has tried to employ against your life, realize that you are important to your Heavenly Father.

Bartimaeus heard that Jesus of Nazareth was passing through town, but interestingly, he didn't call for Jesus of Nazareth.

"Jesus, *Son of David*, have mercy on me!" He shouted. When Jesus heard that, He stopped and told Bartimaeus to come to Him (Mark 10:46-49).

It's important that you understand what Bartimaeus did in this passage.

You see, during the final years of Jesus' life, His claim to be the Son of God was very controversial. Many times people attempted to kill Him for saying that He was God's Son. When He traveled to minister in His hometown, His work was hindered because they only viewed Him as Jesus of Nazareth. That means they looked at Him as the human son of Joseph and Mary, but they didn't respect Him or believe that He was the Messiah.

When Jesus began to teach and minister, they all looked at each other and said, "He's just the carpenter's son, and we know Mary, his mother, and his brothers — James, Joseph, Simon, and Judas. All his sisters live right here among us. Where did he learn all these things?" And they were deeply offended and refused to believe in Him (Matthew 13:55-57).

Their refusal to believe in Who He was caused them to lose the rewards of faith they could have received.

Bartimaeus, however, was different. When everyone around him was talking about "Jesus of Nazareth," he made a decision. He called out for Jesus, *Son of David.*

Just choosing to address Jesus as the Son of David was praise in itself. That was the title reserved only for the Messiah Who was to come.

A blind man saw more about Jesus than people who had perfect eyesight.

Bartimaeus was doing more than asking for help. When he shouted out to Jesus, he was essentially saying, "I believe You are Who You say You are. I believe You are the Messiah Who has the power to heal, and I'm asking you to have mercy on me."

I'm sure there were many people calling on Jesus that day. The Bible shows us that throughout His ministry, crowds constantly pressed in on Him hoping to receive something.

Bartimaeus was the only person who shouted Jesus' name in praise and in faith. Notice the result. Jesus stopped, called for Bartimaeus, and said, "What do you want me to do for you?"

Praise is a prescription from Heaven that will eradicate depression and anxiety and bring a steady stream of joy into your atmosphere.

We must realize that Jesus wasn't in Jericho to minister. He wasn't preaching or teaching there. He was passing through on His way to Jerusalem. Bartimaeus wasn't scheduled for a miracle that day, but his praise allowed him to pencil his name in on Heaven's calendar.

If he had not praised Jesus that day, he may have continued to sit on the side of the road as a blind beggar for the rest of his life.

One moment of engaging God in praise caused his life to change forever.

That's the powerful aspect of praise that many miss. It is a weapon given to us by God to activate the power of His presence.

GIANT-KILLING PRAISE

Praise puts God in the driver's seat of your situation. One of the most difficult things we have to do as believers is realize that the battle belongs to the Lord and He will fight on our behalf.

How else would people in the Bible stand against impossible odds and still finish victoriously? It wasn't because of their natural strength or ability; it was the anointing of God in their life and His presence intervening on their behalf.

Consider how insane it sounded for David, a mere shepherd boy, to stand in front of Goliath, a seasoned warrior, and mock him.

He shouted out, "Today the Lord will conquer you, and I will kill you and cut off your head. And then I will give the dead bodies of your men to the birds and wild animals, and the whole world will know that there is a God in Israel! And everyone assembled here will know that the Lord rescues his people, but not with sword and spear. This is the Lord's battle, and he will give you to us!" (1 Samuel 17:46-47).

Why could a young man who was a shepherd and songwriter stand and contest a giant while an entire army of men hid in the foothills behind him?

David had developed a life of praise with God that God honored even years after David had died. David's praise had stored up so much favor with God that God still withdrew favors from his account to bless the nation of Israel over 300 years later.

> *For my own honor and for the sake of my*
> *servant David, I will defend this city and*
> *protect it.*
>
> *2 Kings 19:34 NLT*

David should have died that day, but his life of praise protected him and brought him victory that no one else could achieve.

Do you realize that the same love David had for the Lord which inspired him to write psalms was the same love that was offended by Goliath's blasphemy?

The initial reason he stopped and decided to fight Goliath was that he could not endure the blasphemy of the God Whom he so fervently praised.

After David had so thoroughly bragged on God's

power, ability, and strength, God had no choice but to come through and back him up.

David, a man after God's own heart, understood the mind of God and what God wanted from him.

He knew that we were created to worship and praise the Lord. He realized that praise was what God wanted from His people. With that knowledge, He realized God would never disregard someone who constantly gave Him praise and worship.

David dedicated himself to a lifelong journey of praise and worship and reminded the Lord of that dedication in times of trouble:

> *What will you gain if I die, if I sink into*
> *the grave? Can my dust praise you? Can*
> *it tell of your faithfulness?*
> **Psalm 30:9 NLT**

God cannot and will not ignore praise. No matter where we look in Scripture, we find praising people to be victorious people. God always creates a way of escape and victory for them.

THE ENEMIES OF MY ENEMIES . . . ARE MY ENEMIES

Imagine if the U.S. military was running a special mission to eliminate a group of terrorist forces overseas.

A General stands up from his chair and begins to lay out the new plan for his key leaders.

"We feel like our tactics over the years have been very boring, so we've come up with a new strategy we'd like to attempt.

Instead of sending special operations forces into the war zone to engage the enemy, each of you will be trained by a vocal coach. Once we feel that you're 'performance ready' we'll be releasing you into battle.

The first squadron that advances toward our enemy will not be equipped with any weapons. You will simply play your instruments and sing loudly."

Wouldn't you love to see the look on people's faces in the debriefing room when that brand-new set of ridiculous tactics was revealed to the soldiers for the first time? I can't imagine the response.

However, that is exactly what King Jehoshaphat instructed Judah to do when their enemies rose up against them. A vast army was marching against him and declared war against the tribe of Judah.

The next day as they went out to battle, the king appointed singers to walk ahead of the army, singing to the Lord and praising Him.

The Bible says that at the moment they began to sing and give praise, the Lord caused the enemy armies to begin fighting among themselves. They all began to kill one another until the army of Judah arrived at the look-out point in the wilderness. Dead bodies covered the ground as far as they could see. Not a single enemy had escaped (2 Chronicles 20:21-24).

The story continues that as they began to gather the plunder, there were so many valuables it took them three full days to collect it all.

This was a lesson to the tribe of Judah that the battle didn't belong to them, it belonged to the Lord. When we engage in praise unto God, He rises up and fights our battles for us.

As we saw in Psalm 22:3, the very thing that causes God to arise is our praise. When God rises up, every enemy that opposes us must flee.

> *Let God arise, let His enemies be scattered, And let those who hate Him flee before Him.*
>
> *Psalm 68:1 NASB*

It doesn't matter what form your enemy takes, it must flee from you as God arises in your praise. Are you battling sickness or disease? Praise God like Bartimaeus did until you praise your way into healing.

Do you feel locked in a prison of anxiety and fear

throughout your day? Praise God like Paul and Silas did until the doors of the prison came open (Acts 16:25-26).

Don't allow the enemy to weaken you when God has assigned a mighty purpose to your life. Praise your way into overwhelming strength and attack your divine mission with momentum.

If an entire nation can be protected from destruction because of praise, your life will be no different.

Praising people are powerful people. In my book, *Praise. Laugh. Repeat.*, I wrote something that God spoke to me once in prayer: "Praise is a prescription from Heaven that will eradicate depression and anxiety and bring a steady stream of joy into your atmosphere."

When you dedicate yourself to a life of praise, you have decided to live a life of power.

According to His Word, thanksgiving and praise are the two vehicles that bring you into the presence of God. Nothing positions you for divine intervention more quickly than genuine, heartfelt praise.

Don't allow yourself to give voice to the problems and issues the enemy may try to launch at you. Instead, praise God for His goodness and mercies that are new every morning. His faithfulness is great.

CHAPTER 7

THE PROTECTIVE POWER OF YOUR WORDS

"Whoever says to this mountain, 'Be removed and be cast into the sea,' and does not doubt in his heart, but believes that those things he says will be done, he will have whatever he says."
—MARK 11:23 NKJV

My father had just arrived as a freshman at Bible college to study for ministry. In his opening months at the school, he witnessed a prank that was played by a few of the seniors.

Several students decided it would be funny to convince a fellow classmate that he was sick even though he felt fine.

One day, during their duties in the mail room, they began to ask the other student, "Are you okay? You look horrible."

"I feel fine," the student replied. But they insisted that he didn't look well. The student shrugged it off.

Later, the seniors persuaded several of their friends to try to convince him again. "Hey man, is everything okay?" they asked. "You look like you're coming down with something."

"No, I feel fine," he insisted, but he began to look unsure.

That night at dinner, several others approached him and started the same routine, insisting that he must be getting sick. He was looking worried now.

After dinner he retired to his dorm room complaining that he didn't feel well. He stayed in all night.

The next morning he wasn't in classes and missed the next three days because he was sick.

Though admittedly a cruel joke, it shows just how powerful the words you speak and the words you believe really are.

> *Since we have the same spirit of faith according to what has been written, "I believed, and so I spoke," we also believe, and so we also speak,*
> *2 Corinthians 4:13 ESV*

Good or bad, the outcomes of our lives are the result of actions we've taken based upon personal beliefs we hold. Our words are governed by those beliefs. The Bible teaches us that nothing supernatural can be accomplished in our lives without some level of belief. Notice that what you speak comes from the basis of what you believe. That's why it's so important what we choose to accept as truth in our lives.

FACTS VS. TRUTH

I believe that it's possible for something to be a fact but not be truth. Although there are things that may take place in your life that are factual, they may not agree with the Word of God, which is ultimate truth. The apostle John wrote that God's Word is truth that can sanctify us (John 17:17).

For example, there may be a believer who is diagnosed with cancer. The fact is, they have cancer in their body. Truth, however, declares that they were healed of every sickness and disease by the stripes Jesus took upon His back (1 Peter 2:24).

How they react to the ultimate truth of God's Word will determine the facts of their life. Confession plays a major role in appropriating the unseen blessings of God for our lives. More simply, you can have what you say when you speak God's Word.

Everything we see in the universe was created by the mighty Word of God (John 1:1-3).

The materials to build the car you drive and the house you live in came out of God's mouth. Every animal you've ever seen roaming this earth was formed because God spoke a word. In fact, God said that His words carry power to perform at all times.

> *So shall my word be that goes out from my mouth; it shall not return to me empty, but it shall accomplish that which I purpose, and shall succeed in the thing for which I sent it.*
> *Isaiah 55:11 ESV*

Words are not natural things. Because they originated with God, they are spiritual elements with a supernatural root. Jesus was very clear about this when He addressed His disciples. He said:

> *The words that I speak to you are spirit, and they are life.*
> *John 6:63 NKJV*

Many people have never made the connection between what they say and what they have. They have no idea the two are connected.

When God created man, He created him as a mirror image of Himself (Genesis 1:26). He finished by breathing the breath of life, which was His own life force, into the lungs of man making him a living being. We were created to function exactly like God, which includes speaking living words that are full of power. Consider this warning regarding our words:

> **Death and life are in the power of the tongue, and those who love it will eat its fruits.**
>
> **Proverbs 18:21 ESV**

Essentially, this verse is telling us that we are reservoirs of supernatural power and the faucet that releases it into our lives is the words we speak.

This is not, as some have argued, a New Age principle. This is how power has functioned since the beginning of time.

A SKYSCRAPER RISING INTO HEAVEN

At the time after Noah's flood, the whole Earth spoke the same language. The people moved out of the east and into the plain of Shinar and settled there.

Although the Lord had commanded them to spread through the whole Earth and replenish it, they said, "Let's build ourselves a city and a tower that reaches Heaven. Let's make ourselves famous so we won't be scattered here and there across the Earth" (Genesis 11:4).

So they began to build the city of Babel, which later became Babylon, a location that has caused problems for God's people ever since.

Under their leader, Nimrod, the people at Babel began constructing a tower, which they planned to build higher and higher until it reached into Heaven.

That's impossible, you might be thinking. But let's take a look at how God regarded the situation:

> *And the Lord said, "Behold, they are one people, and they have all one language, and this is only the beginning of what they will do. And nothing that they propose to do will now be impossible for them. Come, let us go down and there confuse their language, so that they may not understand one another's speech."*
>
> *Genesis 11:6-7 ESV*

God knew the power of their words had brought such unity that they could accomplish anything they set their hearts to do.

He was forced to confuse their language so that their words could not be understood and their power would be removed. Their words were allowing them to accomplish something that is seemingly impossible. This is a direct result of the God-like quality of our words. They contain power to create.

Supernatural words don't just create something from something else in our physical world. Anyone can do that. Instead, God's Word says that our words create reality from that which is unseen:

> *By faith we understand that the entire universe was formed at God's command, that what we now see did not come from anything that can be seen.*
>
> *Hebrews 11:3 NLT*

The visible realm was created and formed by the invisible realm. Our words are catalysts that trigger supernatural reactions in the natural realm.

THE HIGHEST LEVEL OF FAITH

There are many ways to manifest the power of God. For example, if someone wants to receive healing, God has created multiple ways to release it.

One avenue is for believers to lay hands on the sick and pray for them. According to Mark 16:18, this will bring healing.

The Apostle Paul used another method: handkerchiefs and aprons he laid upon his body, which were then taken and laid upon the sick. When those cloths touched the sick, they were made whole and evil spirits left them (Acts 19:12).

However, the highest level of faith operates by only speaking the Word of God and watching things change in the natural realm.

Once, a Roman soldier approached Jesus and asked Him to heal his servant. "He's lying at home in bed," he said. "He's paralyzed and in terrible pain."

"I'll come and heal him," Jesus replied.

With faith like Jesus had never seen, the soldier said:

> *Lord, I am not worthy for You to come under my roof, but just say the word, and my servant will be healed.*
>
> *Matthew 8:8 NASB*

Immediately, Jesus spoke the word of healing and the servant was healed that very moment (Matthew 8:13).

Notice that Jesus didn't have to take the time to travel to the soldier's house and lay hands on his servant. He spoke one word from where He stood and that word traveled to the servant and healed his body.

SPEAK TO THE THING THAT OPPOSES YOU

Our words don't just affect our bodies and minds, they also have an effect on the world around us.

One day, as Jesus and His disciples were leaving the town of Bethany, He became hungry. Looking up, He noticed a fig tree in the distance.

He walked over to it expecting to eat some of the fruit, but when He got closer He realized there were only leaves on the tree. Seeing that there was no fruit, Jesus spoke and said, "May no one ever eat your fruit again!" (Mark 11:12-14).

In his commentary, Adam Clarke writes, "It has been asked, 'How could our Lord expect to find ripe figs in the end of March?' Answer, Because figs were ripe in Judea as early as the Passover. Besides, the fig tree puts forth its fruit first, and afterwards its leaves. Indeed, this tree, in the climate which is proper for it, has fruit on it all the year round, as I have often seen."[1]

Jesus cursed the tree because it was acting in direct rebellion to its intended purpose. God created the tree to be fruitful, but it was bearing no fruit.

When He and His disciples returned from Jerusalem they passed the fig tree again. Remembering what had happened the day before, Peter exclaimed, "Look, Rabbi! The fig tree you cursed has withered and died!"

Jesus took this opportunity to teach His disciples about the supernatural law of confession. He began to show them that their faith in God gave them authority to speak to things in the natural realm.

> *For assuredly, I say to you, whoever says to this mountain, 'Be removed and be cast into the sea,' and does not doubt in his heart, but believes that those things he says will be done, he will have whatever he says.*
>
> *Mark 11:23 NKJV*

Jesus dropped a bomb on His disciples. He gave them insight into the most powerful level of faith that any believer could possibly walk in . . . and then showed them how to activate it.

When Carolyn and I organized our ministry and submitted the paperwork to launch our nonprofit, we went to see our accountant.

As we sat in her office, we discussed how long it would take to receive IRS approval.

"Well," she said. "It takes quite a while. I have clients who have submitted their nonprofit paperwork to the IRS two years ago and are still waiting to hear anything back. It can take quite some time because they're so busy."

When she said that, I felt faith rise up in my spirit. There was no way that we were going to wait two years to begin what God had called us to do.

We submitted our paperwork to the IRS on the first week of September that year. I began to say, "Before November ends I will hold the approval in my hand."

The enemy tried to make me feel foolish for saying it. He would send thoughts to tell me I couldn't control what was going on in a government office and I would have to wait in line like everybody else.

I persisted. Every time I thought about the situation I would say, "Before November ends I'll hold the approval in my hand."

We were traveling at the end of October and the beginning of November. When we arrived back to Virginia Beach, I went to check the mail. Inside I found a letter from the IRS.

When I opened it, I saw that it was stamped "approved" on November 4th. While others had been waiting for over two years, I received my approval in less than two months. How could that be? It happened like I said because I was operating in the protective power of my words. Jesus said:

By your words you will be justified, and

> ***by your words you will be condemned.***
>
> *Matthew 12:37 ESV*

The words that come out of your mouth can either bring you life or death, justification or condemnation.

The Gospel of Mark tells us about a woman who had suffered for most of her life with internal bleeding. She had gone broke by spending all of her money on medical care. When she heard Jesus was coming through town she used the protective power of her words to draw on the authority of Jesus' healing anointing.

> ***For SHE SAID, "If I touch even his garments, I will be made well." (Emphasis added)***
>
> ***Mark 5:28 ESV***

I want you to notice that in this story, Jesus didn't even know she was there. Unless she pressed through the crowd and took action on her own words, He wouldn't have known she existed.

She defined the freedom of her future by her faith-filled confession. You can access the same supernatural results by taking advantage of the power of your words.

Don't succumb to the belief that you have to take life as it comes. On the contrary, you can determine the course of your life by the power of your words.

The psalmist David understood the importance of guarding your words. Flippant speaking leads to failure. He began to pray and ask God to help him:

> *Set a guard, O Lord, over my mouth;*
> *Keep watch over the door of my lips.*
> **Psalm 141:3 NASB**

Not only did he pray this prayer, he also learned to make faith-filled statements. Although he faced mortal danger many times throughout his life, he said that he would live and not die to declare the works of the Lord (Psalm 118:17).

If you will be faithful to guard your words, you will also guard your life from trouble (Proverbs 21:23).

PUT AN END TO YOUR PERSONAL FAMINE

Your enemy wants you to react to the Word of the Lord with a word of doubt. He wants you to be skeptical. Many times unbelief is realized through the words we speak. From the very beginning of time the enemy's job has been to cause us to doubt the words of God.

When the serpent approached Eve in the Garden of Eden, his first words recorded in Scripture are, "Did

God really say?" (Genesis 3:1). From the outset he was determined to get mankind to doubt the very thing that could give us complete freedom.

During the days of Elisha the prophet there was a famine in the land of Samaria. However, God spoke through Elisha to change the condition of the economy in a single day. In a time of depression and famine food is naturally very expensive, but Elisha prophesied that in one day food prices would drop dramatically and the famine would be over.

The officer assisting the king responded to Elisha's words by saying, "That couldn't happen even if the Lord opened the windows of heaven!"

What a foolish thing to say. If God said it, it's going to come to pass (Numbers 23:19).

Elisha responded to the assistant and revealed the judgment he would experience for doubt-filled words:

> *You will see it happen with your own eyes, but you won't be able to eat any of it!*
>
> *2 Kings 7:2 NLT*

That's the frustration that comes from speaking with doubt rather than aligning your words with God's Word and expecting to receive supernatural blessings.

THE FORMULA FOR VICTORY

God doesn't want you on the outside looking in as everyone else is receiving their blessings from Heaven. Our words are seeds that will produce a harvest for us.

There is no force in hell or on earth that can resist the force of your anointed words.

Many people believe that the blood of Jesus is enough to live an overcoming life, but that's not what the Bible says:

> *They overcame him by the blood of the Lamb AND by the WORD of their testimony. (Emphasis added.)*
> *Revelation 12:11 NKJV*

It's time for us to speak purposeful words that will alter the reality of our lives. Don't just say what everyone else is saying; say what God said in His Word.

Don't fall into the temptation of doubting the Word of God over your life. Take it in and speak it out. You can speak protection over your life, children, loved ones, home, and livelihood.

Remember that you can never be wrong when you say what God has already said.

Speak the Word.

#BLOODONTHEDOOR

CHAMPIONS ARE NOT CREATED TO BE PITIED, THEY'RE CREATED TO BE ENVIED.

PART 2

THE BENEFITS OF COVENANT CARE

CHAPTER 8

THE GATES OF HELL WILL NOT PREVAIL

"I will build my church, and the gates of hell shall not prevail against it."
— MATTHEW 16:18 ESV

It was a cool June night in Salt Lake City, Utah, as almost 20,000 fans filled the Delta Center for Game 5 of the 1997 NBA Finals.

Michael Jordan and the Chicago Bulls had just suffered their second loss against the Utah Jazz, causing the seven-game series to be tied 2-2.

The Jazz had one more game at home before returning to Chicago for the rest of the series and needed to win a third straight game. Otherwise, the odds would be completely stacked in the Bulls' favor.

A piece of news emerged that day that must have brought excitement into the Utah Jazz locker room. Due to flu-like symptoms, Michael Jordan would not be one hundred percent for Game 5.

Would this be the extra momentum the Utah Jazz needed to take the lead in the series?

The press and announcers reported that Jordan had been up all night, in bed all day, hadn't eaten anything, and failed to attend the light practice the team held earlier that afternoon. According to his trainer, this was most likely due to food poisoning from the previous night's dinner.

As he emerged onto the court, his weakness was readily visible. He appeared shaky as the team began to warm up, and close-ups from the camera crew revealed tired, bloodshot eyes.

It didn't look good for the Bulls.

Champions are not created to be pitied, they are created to be envied.

As the game began, the Jazz seemed to relish their home-court advantage and wasted no time dominating the Bulls. At one point in the first half, they held a demoralizing 16-point lead.

About that time, something changed in Michael Jordan. As had happened many times before, something came alive inside of him and he stepped into the zone.

With explosive force he scored 17 points in the second quarter, and finished the game with 38 points total.

In the final moments, he made a three-point shot that

swung the momentum and lead back to the Bulls.

With only a few seconds remaining in the game, the result was safely in the Bulls' favor. Weary from battle, Jordan fell into teammate Scottie Pippen's arms. This iconic image has come to symbolize "The Flu Game."

This gave the Bulls the momentum to return home and win the next game making them the 1997 NBA Champions.

I guarantee none of the members of the Utah Jazz looked at Michael Jordan in pity. Champions aren't created to be pitied, they're created to be envied.

Imagine how foolish you would seem walking into the Bulls' locker room after their final game that year with your head hanging low. Think about the weird looks you'd get as you patted all of them on the backs and said, "There's always next year, guys."

Champions aren't looked down upon; they're looked up to and respected. We as believers are champions. According to the Apostle Paul, God has given us the victory through Jesus Christ our Lord (1 Corinthians 15:57).

The Church was not created to live in defeat and tragedy. We were divinely commissioned to be eternally victorious through the power of Jesus Christ.

We are not supposed to be a struggling, hurting, and broken body of believers, we are called to command in the supernatural realm as kings (Revelation 1:6).

A VICTORIOUS CHURCH

Although it may contradict what some people have been taught about the Church, we have been anointed and raised to power by Christ's resurrection.

It's dangerous to confuse humble and meek with afflicted and weak. There's not a chance that the Church at large will fail. It was Jesus Who said:

> *I will build my church, and all the powers of hell will not conquer it.*
> *Matthew 16:18 NLT*

Another translation of this verse says that the gates of hell will not prevail. So, if the gates of hell aren't prevailing, then it's the Church who is prevailing.

Christ was very clear that the Church would be a driving force on this earth in the last days. He called us the light of the world and said that a city set on a hill cannot be hidden (Matthew 5:14).

If we are a city that is set on top of a hill, the world should never be looking down at us, they should always be looking up to us.

As Kenneth Hagin once wrote, "If you're not looking down on the devil, you're not high enough."[1]

The prophet Micah shows us a picture of what the

Church will look like when it is completely unhindered by the forces of hell. This passage gives us insight into God's perfect will for the functionality of His church:

> *In the last days, the mountain of the Lord's house will be the highest of all— the most important place on earth. It will be raised above the other hills, and people from all over the world will stream there to worship. People from many nations will come and say, "Come, let us go up to the mountain of the Lord, to the house of Jacob's God. There he will teach us his ways, and we will walk in his paths."*
>
> **Micah 4:1-2 NLT**

God's desire is to set His children above all things. I cannot stress this point enough. In the final days, the Lord's house will be the highest of all.

When Christ was resurrected, had ascended into Heaven, and was seated at the right hand of God, we were also raised and seated *far above* every evil thing in this world (Ephesians 1:20-22; 2:5-6).

A verse of Scripture that I had read hundreds of times but never saw the true power of is John 3:31. Take a look at this powerful revelation that will change your perspective:

> *He who comes from above is above all.*
> *He who is of the earth belongs to the*
> *earth and speaks in an earthly way. He*
> *who comes from heaven is above all.*
>   *John 3:31 ESV*

If you come from above, you're above all! At one time Jesus was the only person on the earth Who had come from above. Now, as we saw from Paul's letter to the Ephesians, we are also seated in heavenly places with Christ. We now come from above and are above all.

DRIVE THE CAR

I'm surprised at the number of people who accept the fact that there are many details that must be acknowledged in order to have success in life, but are frustrated that supernatural success doesn't come easily.

Natural success and strength require proper nutrition, sleep, exercise, study, and diligent work, just to name a few things.

It would be foolish to sit in your car and become angry when, after half an hour, you were still in your driveway. Yes, the car has the power and ability to take you where you need to go, but there are steps you must take to make it work. First, you must put gas in the tank. Next, you must start the engine. Finally, you've got to put the car in gear and begin to drive.

In the same way, proper steps must be taken to experience supernatural success.

> *If you fully obey the Lord your God and carefully keep all his commands that I am giving you today, the Lord your God will set you high above all the nations of the world.*
>
> *Deuteronomy 28:1 NLT*

Notice that the level of your obedience to God's commands will determine how high you are raised. Does this mean that every time you fail to obey one of God's commands you have to leave your seat in heavenly places and come back to a lower spiritual level?

No, but understand that the benefits of being seated on a heavenly level are only realized by being obedient to God's instructions.

In the Old Testament, God spoke to Joshua, whom He used to destroy the walls of Jericho, and told him the exact same thing. Joshua was not even at the level we are as believers. Jesus hadn't yet come to the earth and died. There was no way for Joshua to be seated in heavenly places, but he was still mightily used by God because of this principle.

If he would be willing to do all that was written in the Word of God, he would become prosperous and successful (Joshua 1:8).

Did you know that the Bible says that the greatest man who lived prior to Christ's resurrection was John the Baptist, but the least person in the New Testament, including any one of us, is greater than he was? (Matthew 11:11).

The benefits of being seated on a heavenly level are only realized by being obedient to God's instructions.

The reason Jesus said that is because regardless of how much power in which any righteous man or woman operated during the Old Testament, it wasn't even close to what has been given to us in the New Testament.

God has chosen to glorify His children so that we may bring glory to God. God not only glorified Jesus, but He chose to glorify us who belong to Him.

> *Those whom he justified he also glorified.*
> *Romans 8:30 ESV*

You have been empowered by the Holy Spirit to be a vital part of the victorious church.

In the following chapters, I want to show you that you are not called to be pitied in any area of your life. You should be envied by this world.

The power of God's protective covenant stretches to cover all of the details of your life, family, business, and future. It's truly a supernatural blessing to be connected to a God Who cares so deeply for His children.

As a champion through Jesus Christ, your life should be cause for celebration and not mourning. Although you may have experienced loss and crisis in the past, declare that from this day forward you will begin to take advantage of the wonderful promises of God.

CHAPTER 9

DIVINE PROTECTION FOR YOUR FUTURE

*"And if I go and prepare a place for you, I will come
again and will take you to myself, that where I am
you may be also."*
—JOHN 14:3 ESV

One thing that has become readily evident to me in the past few years is that Christians and non-Christians alike are very concerned about the future. Specifically *their* future.

Many Americans spend up to $10 a minute to speak to a psychic on the phone in the hopes of hearing some advice that will help them in the future. Visiting a psychic in person can cost anywhere from $200 to $500 an hour.

I've often wondered why, if psychics can predict the future and can help others be successful, so many of them have to house their businesses in run-down hovels in the ghetto. (Just a thought.)

According to Dr. Robin-Marie Shepherd, a researcher

at Auckland University in New Zealand, psychic phone line addicts are spending on average almost $27,000 a year to seek guidance on their finances, their love lives, and other burning issues.[1]

Hollywood capitalizes on our desire to know the future by predicting what it might be like. For example, *Armageddon* and *2012,* two movies with apocalyptic settings, quickly became box office hits and combined to gross over $1.3 billion worldwide.

It's clear that people are looking for more than a mental escape from the mundane tasks of everyday life. They are concerned with what lies ahead.

God, Who created us and knows our innermost desires, said that He would reveal secrets about the future when we ask Him in prayer (Jeremiah 33:3).

He gave us that promise because He understood that the human spirit is created with an inherent desire to have knowledge of future events.

JUDGMENT IS COMING

The Bible is clear that a final judgment will eventually come to the earth. This time of judgment is referred to as the Tribulation.

During this seven-year period, terrible punishments will be released throughout the earth as a result of people rejecting Jesus Christ as their Savior.

As the Antichrist takes power and establishes his demonic rule on the earth, Jesus will begin to release judgments from Heaven. (See Revelation 4-18).

However, there is good news! The Bible teaches that Jesus is coming back to remove His people from the earth and take us to Heaven.

Sadly, many Christians cannot agree as to when this will happen in regard to the Tribulation. Will we as believers have to stay here for part or all of the judgment, or will we be removed from the earth before it begins? As respected eschatology scholar Dr. Mark Hitchcock once asked, "When will the believing be leaving?"[2]

Although there are three main views as to when Christians will be raptured and taken to Heaven, it is my belief that only one of these positions makes sense scripturally.

While there are some who believe that Christians will endure half or all of the Tribulation, I'm going to show you five reasons from Scripture that create a strong argument that we will be removed from the earth before even one of God's judgments is released.

Obviously, this is a much larger topic than I can properly cover within the confines of one chapter. For further reading and study on this subject, I recommend *The End*, Dr. Mark Hitchcock's definitive book on end times prophecy or *Things to Come* by J. Dwight Pentecost. (Not for the faint of heart.)

These next five sections will show you why those who have the blood of Jesus on their doors can expect to be exempted from the divine wrath of the Tribulation.

1. THE ABSENT CHURCH

The Bible is a divine guidebook from God. He loves His children more than we could ever imagine. Scripture gives us countless instructions to keep us from the eternal damnation of hell, sickness and disease, sadness, poverty, lack, and many other evil things.

The Church is God's prized possession. We are the apple of His eye. You would think that if He knew we would have to endure the coming Tribulation, He would give us some instruction in His Word to guide us safely through that terrible time.

The most detailed description of the Tribulation is found in Revelation chapters 4 through 18. Within those chapters John pens a very vibrant description of the events that will take place on the earth.

The Greek word for the Church is *ekklesia,* meaning "the called out assembly."[3] This word occurs twenty times in the book of Revelation. It is written nineteen times in chapters 1-3 and doesn't appear again until

Revelation 19, where the Church is pictured as a bride returning to the earth with her Bridegroom.

As God is raining down judgments upon the earth, why is His prized possession, the Church whom He loves so much, never mentioned one time?

This sudden disappearance of the Church is very suspicious. The fact that we don't see the Church mentioned again until Christ returns at His Second Coming should be a clue to us that the Church is absent during judgment.

2. THE TWENTY-FOUR ELDERS

So where is the absent Church during judgment? I believe the twenty-four elders spoken of throughout the book of Revelation are a representation of the Church already in Heaven during the Tribulation.

There are three main reasons to support the claim that the elders represent the raptured Church. First, they are seated on thrones (Revelation 3:21). No other beings besides God, Christ, and church-age believers are promised thrones anywhere in Scripture.

Secondly, they are wearing crowns which church-age believers will receive at the judgment seat of Christ. Angels are never pictured wearing crowns, and Old Testament saints will not be resurrected and rewarded until the end of the Tribulation (Daniel 12:1-3). So that leaves the raptured believers as the only ones who could be wearing crowns and standing in the presence of God.

Finally, church-age believers are the only individuals who are able to sing the song of redemption that the twenty-four elders are pictured singing in Revelation chapter 5. Neither angels nor Old Testament saints can sing this song as they've never been redeemed.

It stands to reason that the Church is not mentioned on the earth during the Tribulation because we will already be raptured and in the presence of God.

3. THE DEVIL'S LEASH

In his second letter to the Thessalonians, Paul gives some insight about how end-time events will transpire. God has a time line for His prophetic agenda. Look at what Paul wrote to the Thessalonians.

> *For that day will not come until there is a great rebellion against God and the man of lawlessness is revealed . . . For this lawlessness is already at work secretly, and it will remain secret until the one who is holding it back steps out of the way.*
>
> *2 Thessalonians 2:3, 7 NLT*

Many scholars, including J. Dwight Pentecost, Distinguished Professor of Bible Exposition, Emeritus, at Dallas Theological Seminary, agree that the man of lawlessness Paul is speaking of is the Antichrist.[4]

Paul tells the Church that the identity of this man cannot be revealed until the one who is holding him back is moved out of the way. The Greek word *katecho* here means "to hold back or restrain."[5] The one who is holding the Antichrist back is "the restrainer."

While many ideas have been proposed through the ages as to who this restrainer is, there are two clues I want to focus on that will help us identify the restrainer.

First, the restrainer must be removable so that the Antichrist may proceed with his evil purpose. Second, the restrainer must be powerful enough to hold back the outbreak of evil under the Antichrist.

Obviously, only the power of the Holy Spirit is sufficient to hold back the power of Antichrist, but as the Holy Spirit is omnipresent, He cannot be removed from any location. In addition, many will be saved during the Tribulation (Revelation 7:9-14). The Holy Spirit's convicting, drawing, and regenerating power is necessary for anyone to be saved.

For these two reasons I believe the Bible is speaking of the Holy Spirit's power working in the believers who make up the Church. The Church, empowered by the

Holy Spirit, is the restrainer.

Believers, whose job it is to restrain evil as the salt of the earth and the light of the world, must be removed for the Antichrist to be revealed, take power, and begin his reign of terror on the earth.

According to Christ, all power has been given unto the believer (Luke 10:19), including the power to cast out evil spirits. My father has often asked, "If I were on the earth when the Antichrist took power, what would stop me from flying wherever he was and casting the devil out of him?"

The reason the devil hasn't been able to progress to the level of world domination yet is because the Church is still here to thwart his plans.

The event that marks the beginning the Tribulation period is the signing of a peace treaty the Antichrist makes with the nation of Israel (Daniel 9:27).

If he's already an established leader to begin the Tribulation, it makes sense that the Church must already be raptured by that point in time.

4. WHO IS JUDGMENT FOR?

Without question, the entire Tribulation period is a terrible judgment against a rebellious world who rejected the Son of God.

The Tribulation in its entirety represents the ultimate wrath of God from which believers are exempt according to Scripture (1 Thessalonians 1:10).

It should be noted that in every type and shadow throughout the Bible, those who were righteous were spared from judgment.

Noah and his family were the only righteous people left on the earth in their generation. Not only were they all spared from the effects of the flood, every one of them was safely in the ark before the first drop of rain fell from the sky (Genesis 7).

Lot and his family, who were living in the wicked city of Sodom and Gomorrah, escaped the town completely before any fire rained down from Heaven (Genesis 19).

In Christ's parable about the wheat and the weeds, He shows a clear picture of separation before judgment. In the field, which represents the earth, wheat (God's people) and weeds (those who reject God) grow together until the time of harvest. When the harvest takes place (the Rapture) the wheat is placed in the barn (Heaven), and the weeds are bound in bundles to be burned (the Tribulation and ultimately in Hell).

Notice that no judgment was dealt out to anyone until after the harvest and separation took place. (See Matthew 13:24-30).

It's clear that judgment doesn't belong to God's people. In the New Testament, Jesus took our punishment and became the subject of God's wrath on the cross. Our sins were paid for by the blood of Jesus.

It would be unjust for God to make Jesus endure the fullness of His wrath on our behalf and then pour judgment out on us anyway.

Our faith in Christ gives us an exemption from divine wrath. The Tribulation is not designed for us and we are not required to participate in any part of it.

5. A HOPE FOR THE FUTURE

Jesus knew that as the time of His return drew close, the world would be in worse shape than ever. He prophesied that in the last days, the world would once again fall into the pattern that was seen in the generations of Noah and Lot (Luke 17:26-30).

As it was in those Old Testament times, people would be living life and going about their business with a clear disregard for God's principles. Wickedness would abound.

When that happens, God reveals Himself to humanity in a new way and humanity is responsible to conform to that revelation. When humanity fails and rebels, God brings judgment and establishes a new period of probation under a new administration.

This concept is called *dispensationalism*, a view held by many great men of God such as John Nelson Darby, who produced an English translation of the Bible based on the Hebrew and Greek texts, D.L. Moody, the great American evangelist and revivalist, as well as the previously mentioned J. Dwight Pentecost.

It's important to understand this concept because Jesus prophesied it would happen again after the grace of the New Testament church age.

Whereas Adam and Eve's season ended with their expulsion from the Garden of Eden, and Noah's season ended with the Great Flood, the season (or dispensation) of grace will end with the Rapture of the Church and the Great Tribulation.

So we must recognize that although there is a coming judgment, we have the wonderful promise of escape from the divine wrath of God.

That's why after describing the events of the Rapture, the Apostle Paul concludes by gently reminding believers to "encourage one another with these words" (1 Thessalonians 4:18).

The hope of the Rapture is encouraging and uplifting for troubled hearts. It's a blessing and a consolation for the people of God.

What kind of encouragement would it be to know you have to endure three and a half or possibly seven years of judgment before you could go to Heaven? Obviously, that's no encouragement at all. In fact, it would promote a feeling of dread for the believers living in the final generation.

The Rapture is a blessing promised to God's people that keeps us from divine wrath for all time. If the blood of Jesus is on your door, you can be sure that you're not just protected from the danger of this age, but also the age to come.

It's wonderful to know that because Jesus shed His blood for us, we are no longer facing the wrath and judgment of God; rather the eternal blessings of Heaven await God's chosen people.

No one has said it better than the Apostle Paul when he wrote an encouragement to the Thessalonians:

> *For God has not destined us for wrath,*
> *but for obtaining salvation through our*
> *Lord Jesus Christ,*
>
> *1 Thessalonians 5:9 NASB*

CHAPTER 10

DIVINE PROTECTION FOR YOUR MISSION

"In My name they will cast out demons; they will speak with new tongues; they will take up serpents; and if they drink anything deadly, it will by no means hurt them."
—MARK 16:17,18 NKJV

In 1855, a bubonic plague pandemic began in the Yunnan province of China.[1] The bacterial infection caused fever, headaches, and vomiting, followed by swollen and painful lymph nodes.

The plague was initially caused by bites from infected fleas and rodents in Asia. Due to trade vessels carrying infected humans, rats, and fleas across the ocean, the disease spread to every inhabited continent killing more than 12 million people in India and China alone.[2]

The disease was extremely contagious. The bubonic form of the plague would spread to the lungs and become pneumonic in nature.

As a victim would cough or sneeze, infected droplets would be released and transmitted from human to human without the involvement of fleas or animals. After death, even the foamy sputum that would form on the corners of the mouth of the victim was still quite contagious.

By the early 1900s, the disease had spread to South Africa and began to claim many lives. Fear of the contagion was so widespread, "you couldn't hire people for $1,000 to bury the dead."[3]

In January of 1910, Dr. John G. Lake, the mighty, miracle-working apostle, returned to South Africa with his missionary party and founded the Apostolic Church.[4]

He began to minister as the bubonic and pneumonic plagues were raging in that nation. He relates the story in his own writings:

> Now watch the action of the law of life. Faith belongs to the law of life. Faith is the very opposite of fear . . . Consequently, the emanation of the Spirit destroys disease germs.
>
> And because we were in contact with the Spirit of life, I and a little Dutch fellow with me went out and buried many of the people who had died from the bubonic plague. We went into the homes and carried them out, dug the graves and put them in. Sometimes we would put three or four in one grave.

We never took the disease. Why? Because the knowledge that the law of life in Christ Jesus protects us. That law was working . . .

[During that time] they sent a government ship with supplies and a corps of doctors.

One of the doctors sent for me and said, "What have you been using to protect yourself? Our corps has this preventative and that, which we use as protection, but we concluded that if a man could stay on the ground as you have and keep ministering to the sick and burying the dead, you must have a secret. What is it?"

I answered, "Brother that is the 'law of the Spirit of life in Christ Jesus.' I believe that just as long as I keep my soul in contact with the living God so that His Spirit is flowing into my soul and body, that no germ will ever attach itself to me, for the Spirit of God will kill it."

He asked, "Don't you think you had better use our preventatives?"

I replied, "No, but doctor I think you would like to experiment with me. If you will go over to one of these dead people and take the foam that comes out of their lungs after death, then put it under the microscope you will see masses of living germs. You will find that they are alive until a reasonable time after a man is dead. You can fill my hand with them and I will keep it under the microscope, and instead of these germs remaining alive, they will die instantly."

They tried it and found it was true. They questioned, "What is that?"

I replied, "That is 'the law of the Spirit of life in Christ Jesus.' When a man's spirit and a man's body are filled with the blessed presence of God, it oozes out of the pores of your flesh and kills the germs."[5]

Dr. Lake believed that because the blood of Jesus had been applied to the door of his life, the supernatural power of Christ was at work within him.

He hadn't traveled to South Africa on a whim. He didn't just pick up one day and decide to become an apostle to another continent.

God had spoken to him, called him, and supernaturally provided the funds for him to set out on his call. That's important. As we discussed in chapter 3, divine direction is one of the main prerequisites for divine protection.

Dr. Lake was operating directly inside his divine calling from God. As a result, no evil thing could harm him. Dr. Lake worked in harsh environments overseas that were sometimes very deadly. The power of God working in his life was no coincidence.

In 1920, ten years after the bubonic plague episode, African fever ravaged the area in which he lived, and in less than a month, one-quarter of the population died.

Agencies of every description were called into action to combat the epidemic. Dr. Lake worked there with several assistants, four of whom died of the fever, but he was never touched by the disease.[6]

Supernatural protection is afforded to you when you're engaged in your own personal mission from God and the blood of Jesus is on the doorpost of your life.

THE ARMOR OF YOUR ASSIGNMENT

After His resurrection, Jesus appeared to His disciples and gave them a supernatural assignment that extends to every New Testament believer. We know it as the Great Commission.

He began by telling them what they were to do and finished by describing the protection that would be provided for them.

> *"... they will pick up serpents with their hands; and if they drink any deadly poison, it will not hurt them; they will lay*

*their hands on the sick, and they will re-
cover."*

Mark 16:15-18 ESV

Notice what Jesus was saying. As long as they remained involved in their purpose, this protective power
would be active in their lives.

These verses were literally fulfilled in the life of the
Apostle Paul. In the final chapter of the book of Acts,
Paul landed on the island of Malta after being ship-
wrecked.

It was cold and rainy when he arrived with his com-
panions, so the native people built a fire. When Paul
grabbed a handful of sticks and put them on the fire, a
poisonous viper, driven out by the intense heat of the
flames, emerged and bit his hand.

When the natives saw the snake fasten itself to Paul's
hand, they expected him to swell up and die from the
deadly venom released by the bite.

Instead, Paul shook the snake off into the flames and
suffered no harm. Not only did he remain alive, his
hand experienced no swelling (Acts 28:1-6).

Although chapter 28 is the final chapter of the Acts
of the Apostles, there is no termination, or conclusion.
Why? Because the acts of the apostles aren't yet finished. Our lives are the continued story of the power of

God being released on the earth.

As missionary statesman Lester Sumrall wrote in his book, *The Believer's Handbook*, "You are part of Acts 29. The Church today is right on schedule in the divine pattern to get the gifts of the Spirit functioning in their fullness. That last unfinished chapter of Acts is still being written."[7]

This means that as you begin to do what God has called you to do, the same divine protection is available for you right now.

THE PLANE THAT COULDN'T CRASH

I recently read a very faith-building story. Heather, a student at Rhema Bible Training College, was returning to Tulsa, Oklahoma, on a small, eight-passenger airplane after a business trip.

As the plane approached the airport, she could see the red and white flashing lights of emergency vehicles on the runway.

Just then, the pilot announced over the intercom that the plane's right-side landing gear would not come down. The pilot went on to say that because the crosswinds were so strong, there was a good chance the plane would flip over when they touched down. He told the passengers to prepare for a crash landing.

The other passengers on board panicked. One man began repeating a Hail Mary prayer. Others called their wives, convinced these were their final moments.

Heather unbuckled her seat belt, stood up, and announced, "Listen! I prayed before we got on this plane. I know we're going to land safely with or without landing gear!"

Make no mistake about it, God is interested in carrying you safely through your purpose on the earth.

Heather began praying and praising God until the stewardess told her to sit down because they were getting ready to land.

"Okay," Heather said, but before she sat down she asked the stewardess where the landing gear was located.

"If I'm not mistaken," the stewardess replied, "I believe it's right underneath your feet."

"That's right, devil," Heather responded. "Do you hear that? You're under my feet. In the name of Jesus, come down!"

Heather stomped her foot twice and on the second stomp, the landing gear came down and the plane landed safely on the runway with no issues.

"That was the smoothest landing I've ever been a part of," Heather reported later.[8]

Safety belongs to the child of God who is pursuing

the purpose He has assigned to their life.

I love what the psalmist said regarding God's personal involvement in our safety:

> *For he will order his angels to protect you wherever you go. They will hold you up with their hands so you won't even hurt your foot on a stone.*
> **Psalm 91:11, 12 NLT**

Make no mistake about it, God is interested in carrying you safely through your purpose on the earth. He has a personal investment in your life and it's in His best interest to keep you alive and safe from all harm.

PROVISION FOR YOUR PURPOSE

I have always found it interesting that as the disciples were actively engaged in what they had been commanded to do, God not only protected them physically, but also financially.

I believe Jesus wanted to teach His disciples this lesson of faith. Many of them were established businessmen before they became His disciples and were probably used to calculating the bottom line.

Rather than pulling out a spreadsheet and showing

them their budget for the work of the ministry, Jesus gave them very unorthodox instructions:

> *Now go . . . Don't take any money with you, nor a traveler's bag, nor an extra pair of sandals. And don't stop to greet anyone on the road.*
>
> *Luke 10:3, 4 NLT*

Wait, what? You want us to travel from city to city, preach the gospel, heal the sick, but take no money to eat or get a hotel room?

Jesus was teaching them that as they completed what they had been called to accomplish, He would make sure they were taken care of and had plenty throughout their lives and ministries.

Later, Jesus reminded them of the divine protection they experienced as they obeyed His commands:

> *And [Jesus] said to them, "When I sent you out with no moneybag or knapsack or sandals, did you lack anything?" They said, "Nothing."*
>
> *Luke 22:35 ESV*

"Doubting" Thomas was among the disciples whom

Jesus sent out with the original instructions. So we know that the disciples weren't just being polite in their answer to Christ here.

If there was even one day when they lacked something (a place to sleep, food to eat, or clothes to wear), I'm sure Thomas would have spoken up quickly and pulled out all of his receipts so that he could be reimbursed by the finance department of Jesus of Nazareth Ministries International, Inc.

However, it was clear. They lacked nothing. Supernatural provision followed them wherever they went because they were actively engaged in their mission.

What about Jesus? He didn't have time to get a job with all the work He had to accomplish for the kingdom. How did He survive? How did He pay His bills? How did He have a traveling ministry that supported twelve men and required a treasurer? (Some people argue that Jesus was a poor, homeless man, but I've never met a homeless man who had to employ a full-time treasurer.) The book of Luke, once again, answers the question:

> *Soon afterward Jesus began a tour of the nearby towns . . . He took his twelve disciples with him, along with some women who had been cured of evil spirits and diseases. Among them were Mary Mag-*

> *dalene, from whom he had cast out sev-*
> *en demons; Joanna, the wife of Chuza,*
> *Herod's business manager; Susanna; and*
> *many others who were contributing from*
> *their own resources to support Jesus and*
> *his disciples.*
>
> Luke 8:1-3 NLT

God supernaturally connected people to Christ who gave financially to further His mission. In addition, Christ performed many miracles of provision for Himself, His disciples, and those who came to hear Him teach (See John 6:1-13).

This is a supernatural promise to those who are willing to walk in complete obedience and pursue their call.

In fact, when Jesus began to discuss the topic of natural provision such as clothes, food, and housing, He told His followers not to worry about them.

"Those are the things that dominate the thoughts of unbelievers," He said. "Your heavenly Father already knows all your needs."

I'm sure that left people thinking, *Well, it's great that He knows our needs, but we need to have our needs met.*

So Jesus gave them the key to unlocking a lifetime of unending blessing.

> *Seek the Kingdom of God above all else,*
> *and live righteously, and he will give*
> *you everything you need.*
>
> *Matthew 6:33 NLT*

As the author of the famous sermon *That's My King*, (a message that has been viewed nearly five million times on YouTube), Pastor S.M. Lockridge, put it, "No far-seeing telescope can bring into visibility the coastline of God's shoreless supply."[9]

MILLIONS OF PEOPLE, MILLIONS OF DOLLARS

If you've never heard of Reinhard Bonnke, the mighty missionary evangelist, I strongly encourage you to search his name on YouTube and watch the clips of crusades that he has held in Africa.*

It's very possible that no one in the history of the world has won more people to Jesus than this man.

At the time this book was written, his office had recorded over 74 million salvations through his ministry.[10]

In 2011, my wife and I accompanied my parents to meet with Dr. Bonnke at his Florida headquarters.

---

*In particular, the video *Evangelism in Nigeria* which can be found at https://youtu.be/MBtBHZtdU78

We sat with him at lunch as he told stories of God's power and explained what his ministry was doing around the world.

I will never forget one of the stories he shared with us that day. He began to explain how much it costs to organize a crusade that would reach millions of people within a matter of days.

It was seemingly an impossible task. I'm sure that at the beginning of his ministry, he wondered where he would acquire the finances to complete such significant work for the Lord.

His vision wasn't just to hold one crusade, which would be a very expensive undertaking in itself, but many of them throughout the world. When the task seemed the most impossible, that's when God moved on Dr. Bonnke's behalf.

He began to share with us how God moved upon one man to sow largely into his ministry. The man didn't just give a generous, one-time gift, he attached himself to Bonnke's vision.

"Since the early 1980s," Dr. Bonnke said, "that man has given over $32 million to our ministry."

As the Lord had done for Christ during his earthly ministry, He sent people to assist Dr. Bonnke as he carried out his personal mission.

Imagine for a moment if, after receiving his calling

from the Lord, Dr. Bonnke decided that instead of crusade evangelism, he would focus his efforts on digging wells and bringing clean water to those living in third-world nations.

Do you think that the supernatural provision of God would have come to him? I can tell you the answer is no. Disobedience will always shut down the flow of supernatural assistance from God.

> *Unless the Lord builds a house, the work*
> *of the builders is wasted.*
> *Psalm 127:1 NLT*

Isn't it encouraging to know that no matter what God has called you to accomplish for Him, your protection is already built into your obedience? God doesn't call you to kill you. God always has your best interests at heart and is actively seeking to help you fulfill your destiny.

YOU CAN FINISH WHAT YOU STARTED

Jesus told His disciples that the biggest obstacle to people coming into the kingdom was not the devil fighting to obtain their souls, but the insufficient number of workers available to preach the gospel (Matthew 9:37).

If God is willing that none should perish, and the

only way to be saved is by hearing the gospel preached, it stands to reason that it's in God's best interests to keep His workers alive.

Sometimes, after a believer has died, you'll hear this verse quoted at the funeral:

> **Precious in the sight of the Lord is the death of his saints.**
>
> **Psalm 116:15 ESV**

Then someone will stand up and misinterpret it by saying, "How precious. God needed another flower for His garden in Heaven."

It's as though they believe God reached down and "plucked" their loved one from the earth only to "plant" them in Heaven. I'm sorry to burst those bubbles, but this is simply untrue.

God isn't double minded. He's not going to work against His own purpose. If Jesus instructed His disciples to pray that God would send laborers into the harvest field, God isn't going to respond by *removing* laborers from His field before they can complete their task.

As we take a closer look at that scripture, we see that the word "precious" is the Hebrew word *yaqar*, and it actually means *costly*.

As my father has preached for years, it costs God

something when one of His children leaves the earth. It's an expensive loss for God because there's an overwhelming harvest to gather and a limited number of laborers available to Him.

This is why I believe that God, through the Holy Spirit, will show you things to come in order to protect your life. This was the case for the Apostle Paul.

By the end of his ministry, Paul was on his way to Jerusalem and stopped in Caesarea to stay with Philip the Evangelist.

A few days later, a prophet named Agabus came to the house and gave Paul a message. He took Paul's belt and bound his own feet and hands with it.

"So shall the owner of this belt be bound by the Jewish leaders in Jerusalem and turned over to the Gentiles," he said. It was a warning for Paul.

"I am ready not only to be jailed at Jerusalem but even to die for the sake of the Lord Jesus," Paul replied. (Acts 21:8-14).

When Paul arrived in Jerusalem shortly after this, he was arrested. After revealing his Roman citizenship, he was transferred to Rome where most historians and Bible commentators agree he was beheaded.[11]

Why would Paul knowingly travel to his own death when he was such a dynamic force in forming the early church? Why would he not heed the voice of the Spirit of God and go somewhere else?

During his imprisonment in Rome, Paul pens what many believe was his last letter—Second Timothy. I believe Paul's final words to his son in the gospel will help us understand why he had no hesitation to go to Jerusalem knowing that his arrest, imprisonment, and death were waiting for him.

After spending this letter encouraging Timothy to be a faithful soldier of Christ, he writes of himself:

> *As for me, my life has already been poured out as an offering to God. The time of my death is near. I have fought the good fight, I have finished the race, and I have remained faithful.*
>
> **2 Timothy 4:6, 7 NLT**

Paul had come to the end of his race and his chest had broken the tape at the finish line. He had completed all that God had for him to do.

Why stick around any longer? In fact, Paul struggled with this concept earlier in his writings to the Philippian church. He longed to go and be with Christ in Heaven, but he knew his time had not come and there was more work to be done on earth (Philippians 1:21-24).

Now that he had completed his assignment, he could

go and be with Christ, Whom he longed earnestly to see.

It's encouraging to know that you can live until you complete your assignment. Your enemy doesn't have the right to stop you in the midst of your most important work. You can finish what you started.

Divine protection can be found as we participate faithfully with God's plan for our lives. Our enemy cannot find us because we are hidden with Christ in God (Colossians 3:3).

And even if he could find us, as Paul asked the Romans, *if God is for us, who can ever be against us?*

GOD DOESN'T INTERVENE WHEN HE SEES CRISIS. HE INTERVENES WHEN HE SEES COVENANT.

CHAPTER 11

DIVINE PROTECTION FOR YOUR FAMILY

"How joyful are those who fear the Lord and delight in obeying his commands. Their children will be successful everywhere; an entire generation of godly people will be blessed."
—PSALM 112:1,2 NLT

It was well past midnight and the baseball game that my cousin, evangelist Jonathan Shuttlesworth, was watching had gone into extra innings.

About six months previously he and his wife, Adalis, had become parents to their first child: a precious baby girl named Camila Evangeline.

Suddenly, as the baseball game was coming to a close, the shrill sound of Camila screaming from the bedroom pierced the quiet summer night.

The ferocity of the shriek brought Jonathan to his feet and he ran into the room where Camila had been sleeping. When he arrived by the bed, he looked down to see his daughter, whose eyes had glazed over. Her tongue was swollen inside of her mouth.

Before he could pick her up, Adalis and her sister, Evelyn, rushed into the bedroom and grabbed Camila.

"Oh no," said Evelyn, a registered nurse. "Call 911. She's having an allergic reaction and is going into shock!"

Earlier that day they had introduced Camila to some pureed bananas along with the milk she had been having since birth. Apparently, the bananas had an unexpected effect on her little body.

"Give her to me," Jonathan said. He took Camila in his arms and began walking around the bedroom thanking God that she was healed. He quoted a psalm over her that reads:

> *His [the one who fears the Lord] descendants will be mighty on earth; The generation of the upright will be blessed.*
> *Psalm 112:2 NKJV*

As he prayed he felt peace come over her and knew his prayers had been answered.

"What did you do?" Evelyn asked as he handed Camila back to her and Adalis.

"I just prayed and thanked God," he responded.

"No, but what *else* did you do?"

Jonathan looked down at his daughter. Her eyes were

no longer glazed over, her tongue was not swollen, and she was looking up at him smiling. In just moments God had touched her and made her whole.

"This is a miracle," Evelyn said. She was absolutely right. God's children are entitled to experience His miracle-working power.

Healing is spiritual bread that we can continually feast upon (See Matthew 15:21-28). Jesus didn't teach that if you're lucky you may experience God's power, or that you may only experience it once or twice in your lifetime.

The New Testament paints a picture of our inheritance that was given through the work of redemption.

Healing is one of the main things that Jesus purchased and left to us by the stripes He took upon His back.

When God heals you or your children, it's not because you got lucky. It's not even because a sovereign God Who picks and chooses Who He will bless saw fit to grant your request . . . this time.

It's because healing is your covenant right through Jesus Christ. He already paid for it and you're entitled to take it home with you.

A DEAD BABY LIVES AGAIN

Bishop David Oyedepo, whom I have mentioned before, related a powerful story in his book, *Releasing the*

Supernatural. Shortly after he and his wife, Faith, were married, she became pregnant with their first son.

Bishop Oyedepo was on the road ministering and holding meetings. When he returned home from his trip his wife met him with sad news. She told him that she had a miscarriage while he was away.

"No, it cannot happen," he responded to her. "Can I have my food please?" That was the end of the discussion about it. Her pregnancy continued until full term and their first son was born with no issues.[1]

Wait a minute. Where was the crying and mourning? Why didn't he call all of his friends to agree with him in prayer? He understood that life is in the power of the tongue (Proverbs 18:21), and his family had the right to claim divine protection.

Why did he know that it was impossible for his wife to miscarry? Because God made a promise to His people concerning their babies:

> *You must serve only the Lord your God. If you do, I will bless you with food and water, and I will protect you from illness. There will be no miscarriages or infertility in your land, and I will give you long, full lives.*
>
> *Exodus 23:25,26 NLT*

That promise doesn't just belong to ancient Israel, it's now ours by faith. It's very important to understand that we can claim many of the promises that were made to the nation of Israel in the Old Testament.

Yes, some of the things God said to them were prophetic and were to be fulfilled through them, but their blessings as God's children became ours when we became God's children. In fact, thanks to the work of Christ Jesus, the covenant we have with God is better than the old covenant Israel experienced.

> *But now Jesus, our High Priest, has been given a ministry that is far superior to the old priesthood, for he is the one who mediates for us a far better covenant with God, based on better promises.*
>
> *Hebrews 8:6 NLT*

One of my pet peeves is hearing someone say, "that's Old Testament" after I get finished quoting Old Testament scriptures. It's as though some people believe the Old Testament isn't actually God's Word anymore.

One of the most powerful revelations we can attain as believers is that we are the seed of Abraham and heirs of the blessing God delivered to him (Galatians 3:14).

Jesus gave us a *better* covenant established upon *bet-*

ter promises. Our experience with God today should not be any less glorious than what they experienced then.

If He promised that He would protect their babies even in their mother's wombs, we should understand that He desires to do the same thing for us under this better covenant we have with Him.

Your children were created to serve the Lord and receive the supernatural blessing passed down through your family.

If you're the first Christian in your family tree, then the blessing begins with you. Your children and grandchildren (along with 998 subsequent generations) can live in and experience the blessings of the Lord.

> **Understand, therefore, that the Lord your God is indeed God. He is the faithful God who keeps his covenant for a thousand generations and lavishes his unfailing love on those who love him and obey his commands.**
>
> **Deuteronomy 7:9 NLT**

Should I throw that verse out because it's Old Testament? No way. The same God Who kept His covenant for a thousand generations then, is doing the same thing today. God wants to bless your children.

That fact is not just true of God, it was reflected in the Son of God during His ministry on the earth. He was constantly searching for ways to bless parents and their children.

Jesus wasn't some cranky old man nervously walking around Nazareth ready to explode at the first person who made any noise.

He wasn't some overly-religious wet blanket. He rebuked people who were like that. He was full of joy and love. So much so that children (who always know how to spot and avoid harsh, nasty people) flocked to Him wanting to talk and spend time with Him.

Furthermore, Jesus wanted them there. He never said, "Go play somewhere else; this is church business."

Instead, He called them over, laid His hands on them, and blessed them (Mark 10:16).

Once, when He and His followers had been in the wilderness for hours and they became hungry, a little boy decided to give his lunch to Jesus rather than eat it himself (John 6:9).

God doesn't reserve His supernatural power until we hit crisis mode. He manifests His goodness to fulfill our daily needs.

What hungry little kid do you know who would be mature enough to give his lunch away? This was one of the many children who loved Jesus—because Jesus loved them.

The story ends with Jesus feeding every family (including the children) until they were so full they couldn't eat another bite.

It was just Jesus revealing His wonderful nature yet again. Notice that He didn't just protect those families from starvation. He made sure they didn't even miss a meal.

That shows us that God doesn't reserve His supernatural power until we hit crisis mode, but instead manifests His goodness to fulfill our daily needs (Matthew 6:11). He truly is good all the time.

HOW TO RUIN A FUNERAL

Jesus loved families so much that one day, He decided to ruin a funeral. Shortly after healing the servant of a Roman officer, Jesus traveled to the village of Nain.

A funeral procession was emerging from the town as He approached the city gates. The young man who had died was a widow's only son.

When he saw her crying as she followed the procession, His heart overflowed with compassion.

"Don't cry," He said. Then He walked over and touched the coffin. The bearers stopped and He told the young man to get up.

The boy sat up, began to talk, and Jesus gave him back to his mother (Luke 7:11-17).

Jesus loved that family so much that He couldn't stand to see that woman all alone.

Smith Wigglesworth, the mighty British evangelist, was a great man of faith. His faith caused him to do amazing things for the kingdom of God.

Taking his cue from Jesus, it's reported that he raised from the dead at least fourteen people, and some say as many as twenty-three.

The story is told that he once entered a funeral home during a viewing. The man who lay in the coffin had been dead for three days, fully embalmed.

Wigglesworth felt faith rise up in his heart and he went into the room where the man was lying and closed the french doors behind him.

Although he was alone in the room, his booming voice could be heard by the people who were in the house. He grabbed the stiff body of the dead man and, holding him by the lapels of his suit, pulled him out of the coffin.

He stood the body up against the wall, took a few steps back and shouted, "Live in Jesus' name!"

The corpse slid down the wall and fell stiffly to the floor. Not deterred, Wigglesworth walked back over, picked him up, and stood him against the wall again.

Standing back he shouted again, "Live in Jesus' name!" As before, the dead man slid down and fell to the floor.

Finally, full of faith, he repeated the procedure and stood back a final time. "Live in Jesus' name!" he boomed. The man coughed and came back to life.

Moments later the french doors opened and Wigglesworth and the formerly dead man came walking out into the parlor of the house arm in arm.[2]

Imagine receiving a loved one back into your family after knowing they were dead and gone. It's amazing the lengths God will go to bless a family.

YOU CAN'T BE PAST YOUR PRIME

God isn't only interested in blessing children and little babies. He has great interest in blessing and protecting every one of His children, no matter their age.

One of the greatest lies we've been made to believe is that as we get older our bodies will break down and become weak.

God has a plan for you to steadily increase in every area of life. Consider this verse:

> *But the path of the righteous is like the*
> *light of dawn, which shines brighter and*

brighter until full day.
                              Proverbs 4:18 ESV

You have been ordained to shine brighter and brighter. In other words, you are set apart to steadily increase until you have finished your race.

You can live a long, full life and accomplish your purpose with force and momentum.

God said that He would cause man's days to be 120 years on the earth (Genesis 6:3). That doesn't mean you're supposed to be 120 years old, sitting in a nursing home, eating vanilla pudding, and playing gin rummy until your 7:00 p.m. bedtime.

It means that God will give you supernatural strength to continue working for Him even in your old age. Look at this description of Moses:

> *Moses was 120 years old when he died, yet his eyesight was clear, and he was as strong as ever.*
> *Deuteronomy 34:7 NLT*

Did you see that? You don't have to be sick or diseased to die. Moses died when he was as strong as ever. Not weak and hobbling around smelling like moth balls. Don't let the enemy lie to you and tell you that you're too old to do anything else for God.

He'll tell you that it's time to leave it to a younger generation. You need to sit back and relax. You have become irrelevant and useless.

What a lie.

When Israel was ready to enter into their Promised Land, Moses sent twelve spies to bring back a scouting report. When they returned, ten of the spies reported all of the impossibilities they had noted.

"The people there are powerful," they said. "Their towns are large and fortified. We even saw giants there!"

Then Caleb, one of the spies, stepped forward and tried to quiet the people. "Let's go at once to take the land," he said. "We can certainly conquer it!" (See Numbers 13).

Fast forward forty-five years. Caleb is now eighty-five years old and it's time for him to claim the land that God promised him. The only problem? Giants were still living in the Promised Land.

Most of us can't fathom an eighty-five-year-old man wielding a sword and going into battle against giants. It's just not done.

Caleb, however, was not just willing to do it, he seemed excited also.

"Today I am eighty-five years old," he announced. "I am as strong now as I was when Moses sent me on that journey, and I can still travel and fight as well as I could then. So give me my Promised Land!" (See Joshua 14).

Imagine having to wait forty-five years to receive the promise God made to you.

Some of you who are reading this book can identify with that. Maybe God gave you a dream or vision for your life many years ago and it still hasn't come to pass yet. I want to encourage you. Your story isn't over. God is faithful to do what He promised He would accomplish through you.

> *For as many as are the promises of God,*
> *in Christ they are [all answered] "Yes."*
> *So through Him we say our "Amen" to*
> *the glory of God.*
>
> *2 Corinthians 1:20 AMP*

God has protected you, as He did for Caleb, and brought you to this point to fulfill His promises to you. It's not too late to act on God's promises and manifest His glory in your life and family.

NOTHING LESS THAN THE BEST

God wants His children to have the best. As my uncle, Pastor Terry Shuttlesworth, has hilariously pointed out,

Toasty-Os are not Cheerios, and Fruity Rings don't taste like Froot Loops.

You might save 79¢ at the grocery store, but you're not fooling anyone. There's a great difference (though I hate to admit it) between the quality of meat at McDonald's and Ruth's Chris Steak House.

Some mothers won't even let their kids eat hot dogs because they can't bear to think what's inside them. (I'm looking at you, Carolyn.)

Obviously, it all comes down to love. If you love your children, you want the best for them. In the same way, God doesn't want you to struggle throughout your life. He doesn't want your body to be filled with things He never planned for you to have, like cancer and diabetes.

He wants to guard you because He loves you.

That's why covenant protection has been extended to your family. You and your children are entitled to live long lives without accident or calamity because you belong to God and the blood of Jesus Christ is on the doorpost of your house.

The devil can huff and puff all he wants to, but he doesn't have the spiritual strength to blow your house down . . . especially now that it's built on the Rock.

CHAPTER 12

DIVINE PROTECTION FOR YOUR MIND

*"Then you will experience God's peace, which exceeds any-
thing we can understand. His peace will guard your hearts
and minds as you live in Christ Jesus."*
—PHILIPPIANS 4:7 NLT

Years ago, when I was a youth pastor, I would take my
youth group to camp every summer. One year, I found
a camp nestled deep in the woods of Virginia and made
plans to take the group there for our event.

When I went to inspect the camp and sign the paperwork, I noticed they had a large, ominous-looking,
plantation-style manor house on the grounds.

Because I'm ornery and love to play practical jokes, I
realized that this would be a wonderful setting to play a
prank on my youth group. (Horrible. I know.)

Later that summer, as we drove the students to the
camp in the fifteen-passenger vans we rented, I spun the
tale of "the haunted manor house, the insane asylum,
and the missing kids."

"Back in the 80s," I began, "there was an insane asylum across the river from the camp we're going to. Several of the patients escaped.

During that time, kids who were staying at the camp sneaked out of their dorms and went into the woods one night and were never found again." I told the story as seriously and gravely as possible.

At first, the kids laughed and took it as a joke, but when they saw I wasn't smiling, they became more apprehensive and I could see the wheels begin to turn in their minds.

I figured at the least the story would keep me and the counselors from having to deal with kids sneaking out at night . . . and man was I right.

I told them all about the manor house that no one could live in because of all the strange things that took place inside. I really set the tone so that when we arrived and they saw that old house looming overhead, it only solidified the strength of my story.

One night, after the service was over and we were hanging out around the campfire, I decided to take them on a tour of the camp. This was the big moment.

We all piled into one of the vans and I began to slowly drive around the camp while I narrated as their tour guide.

Instead of turning on the headlights to illuminate our

tour, I only activated the running lights, casting an eerie, yellow glow on everything.

Unbeknownst to the students, I had sent all the counselors to hide in the woods and around the manor house. As we drove, I retold the story, adding a bit of flair by jamming on the brakes now and then, insisting I saw something move in the woods.

The students in the van were so completely silent that unless you turned around to see them, you wouldn't have known they were there.

Finally, we approached the long, winding driveway of the manor house. Now there was a bit of a buzz in the vehicle. The picture I had painted in their minds had made them jumpy. The sounds of nervous laughter and muffled squeals filled the van.

We arrived at the top of the driveway by the porch and I convinced one brave student to get out and check the basement window. I was sure I'd seen a light turn on or something . . .

He jumped out and slowly approached the house with his eyes darting back and forth. It was in that perfect moment that I gave a silent signal to the hidden counselors who came roaring out of the woods and from behind the house.

I can tell you from experience there is no sound louder than the screams of terrified teenage girls (and boys).

The young man dove back into the van and we peeled out and drove away from the house. I turned around to see over forty kids huddled in the back two rows of a fifteen-passenger van.

Later that night, I walked through the boy's dorm and saw one of our younger students sitting up in his top bunk. He was holding a bottle of Mountain Dew, rocking back and forth, and staring into space.

I had to go over and make sure he understood it was all just a joke and none of the stories were true. After a few minutes of calming him down (and realizing my prank may have gone too far), I gained a new level of understanding about the power of the mind.

Something that wasn't even true had the ability to transport people into a state of fear and anxiety.

Don't get me wrong, nobody was seeking psychiatric counseling after the camp ended, but something as small as a story carried their imaginations to a place where they believed they might be in real danger.

That's why I want to finish by giving you what I believe may be the most important element within this *Blood on the Door* message.

I want to focus on the power of your mind.

It's vital that we understand every person is made up of three parts: spirit, soul, and body. The Apostle Paul made this distinction in his first letter to the Thessalo-

nian church (1 Thessalonians 5:23). I explained this concept in detail in my book *Praise. Laugh. Repeat.*:

> **Your Spirit** is your eternal being. This is the part
> of you that will live eternally in either Heaven or
> Hell. Once you become a Christian, this part of
> you always wants to obey the voice and Word of
> God (Romans 7:15).
>
> **Your Body** is what you see in the mirror. It is
> the natural part of you that is growing older and
> slowly decaying, no matter how much make up,
> perfume, cologne or Axe Body Spray you use.
>
> No matter how long you are a Christian, your
> natural body will always want to sin in some
> way. The Bible says that your body (flesh) will
> constantly be at war with your spirit (Galatians
> 5:17).
>
> So how in the world are we supposed to be vic-
> torious with this system in place? It is the final
> part of you that makes the difference.
>
> **Your Soul** is made up of your mind, your will
> and your emotions. This is the part of you that
> you can change for the better. Your soul can be
> your best friend, empowering you to do what is
> right, or your worst enemy, constantly harassing
> your life. The Bible says that a person becomes

what they imagine in their heart (Proverbs 23:7).

Because of this truth, I believe your soul is the part of you that requires the most maintenance. After all, your body can only do what your mind instructs it to do.

In an earlier chapter we dealt with the power of your words. While it's absolutely true that your words carry supernatural power, the answer to changing the reality of your life doesn't just lie in choosing to speak life-giving words.

In fact, that cannot happen on its own. The Bible is very clear about the process of your words and actions:

> *A good person produces good things from the treasury of a good heart, and an evil person produces evil things from the treasury of an evil heart. What you say flows from what is in your heart.*
> *Luke 6:45 NLT*

We must realize that in order to speak life-giving words that will loose divine protection, our hearts must be filled with the faith to do so.

It may seem like an impossible task to remain full of faith in a world that has been polluted with so much fear, doubt, and unbelief.

God's Word, however, has given us a method to stay full of faith and guard our minds from the pollutants that would act as obstacles to our supernatural success.

Although the entire Bible is full of eternal wisdom, the book of Proverbs was specifically written to give us divine wisdom (Proverbs 1:1-7).

These proverbs were written by Solomon who had greater wisdom than any man. As the New Living Translation says, his wisdom was "as vast as the sands of the seashore" (1 Kings 4:29-31).

So when a man who is wiser than anyone else is giving us secrets of success for life and says, "above all else," our ears should perk up. What he is getting ready to show us is the pinnacle piece of wisdom in his arsenal.

Imagine if the prolific investor Warren Buffett or computer genius Bill Gates said, "I'm going to tell you the number-one secret to my success."

You would listen closely.

Well, guess what? Although Warren and Bill are listed in the top ten wealthiest people in the world every year, their wealth doesn't come close to Solomon's.

In fact, the queen of Sheba made a journey to visit Solomon and see his massive wealth that she'd heard so much about.

Possibly thinking she would impress him, she brought him gifts that would be worth approximately

$100 million today.

When she arrived and saw the level of his wisdom and wealth, it literally took her breath away (1 Kings 10:4-5).

That's the level of success of the man who is about to show us the most important key to life.

Are you ready? This is what Solomon wrote:

> *Guard your heart above all else, for it determines the course of your life.*
> *Proverbs 4:23 NLT*

Guard your heart. The Hebrew word for "heart" in this passage refers to your mind. Although your spirit is a supernatural force that is renewed daily by God (2 Corinthians 4:16), your soul requires protection.

As this is the most important element of success, God must have given us a means to apply it to our lives.

He did.

IT'S TIME TO TAKE PRISONERS

God understands the power of your mind; He created it. He is also aware of the dangers that you face on a daily basis and has given you solutions to solve those problems.

I can't control the thoughts that pop into my mind, you might be thinking. While that might be somewhat true, there is an answer to this issue.

When the Apostle Paul was dealing with the very carnal and immature church at Corinth, he gave them a solution that would get their minds back on track. Understanding, as Christ taught, that the nature of sin and disobedience begins in the unchecked mind, Paul wrote this:

> **We destroy arguments and every lofty opinion raised against the knowledge of God, and take every thought captive to obey Christ,**
>
> **2 Corinthians 10:5 ESV**

While you may not be able to control every thought that "pops into your head," when a thought that is contrary to God's Word comes, you don't have to continually dwell on it.

Take it prisoner. As Paul wrote, make it obey Christ. This is the difference between controlling your mind and being controlled *by* your mind.

The former is an example of a Spirit-led lifestyle, while the latter is a sign of immaturity and is dangerous to your spiritual health. Paul told the Romans, "to be carnally minded is death" (Romans 8:6).

As you search the Scripture, you will find that there are two main ways to ensure that you're controlling (rather than being controlled by) your mind.

When you decide to take control of your thoughts, you will be transformed by the power of God.

STRATEGY ONE: IT'S TIME FOR AN UPGRADE

To me (and many other tech-saavy Americans), there's nothing worse than an old, clunky, unreliable piece of technology.

Almost everyone can relate to the frustration that comes with having an aged, unresponsive computer in the office. It's the one that everyone fantasizes about destroying with a sledgehammer.

It's the copier that never prints straight and all too often jams in moments when you're on a deadline.

Back when cellular phone companies were still operating with two-year contracts, everyone would get excited to renew their contracts because that most likely meant they could also upgrade their phones.

Goodbye old, piece-of-junk iPhone from two years ago. Hello, new, sleek, shiny iPhone (insert upcoming number here).

Sadly, in those days, you couldn't experience the new

features and hardware until you renewed your contract.

In the same way, there are wonderful features and up-grades (like supernatural peace, joy, and love, along with boldness and confidence) that you can experience when you renew your mind.

When you choose to leave your mind in an unre-newed state, you will find yourself conforming to the sinful activities of this world. Paul wrote:

> *And do not be conformed to this world,*
> *but be transformed by the renewing of*
> *your mind.*
>
> *Romans 12:2 NASB*

Transformation comes, not by making your spirit more powerful, but by renewing your mind. After all, your spirit has been united with Christ and all power has been given unto you (Luke 10:19). How do you get more powerful than that?

You can't. Your mind has to be renewed. Otherwise, your mind will side with your flesh and do what it wants to do rather than what your spirit wants to do.

So how does renewal happen?

> *Throw off your old sinful nature and your*
> *former way of life, which is corrupted by*

lust and deception. Instead, let the Spirit
renew your thoughts and attitudes.
Ephesians 4:22-23 NLT

So it's the Spirit of God Who renews your mind. This is done through a supernatural cleaning agent that God always uses: His Word.

The Word of God carries the divine ability to cleanse your mind. Christ uses the Word of God to cleanse His entire body. Paul wrote:

[Christ] gave up his life for [the church]
to make her holy and clean, washed by
the cleansing of God's word.
Ephesians 5:26 NLT

Without a doubt, God's Word is the most protective element you can apply to your mind. When Jesus spent forty days in the wilderness fasting and praying, the devil came often to tempt Him.

Satan wasn't attacking Jesus' spirit, he was tempting His mind. The mind is the battlefield where you must win the war.

Every time the devil came to tempt Jesus and attack His mind, Jesus used the power of God's Word to protect Himself from temptation. The result? His mind was guarded by God's power and He overcame.

Three times in one chapter we have record of Jesus responding to Satan's words by saying, "The Scriptures say" (Luke 4:4, 8, 12).

You have been given divine protection for your mind through the cleansing power of God's Word. His Words are spirit and they are life (John 6:63).

STRATEGY TWO: SET THE TONE

The renewed mind is the weapon that God set at your disposal to continually define the success of your future, so you've got to make sure it's honed and ready to be used for the purpose God has given you.

The Apostle Peter said it best when he wrote, "Prepare your minds for action" (1 Peter 1:13).

Prepare your minds for action. I love that line. It evokes visions of Mel Gibson as William Wallace in *Braveheart,* covered in blue war paint and riding his horse across the battlefield, encouraging the men of Scotland to fight for their freedom. He was preparing them for action.

There is no freedom, including the freedom of your mind, that comes without action. Set the tone of freedom in your mind by taking control of your thoughts.

Fix your thoughts on what is true, and

> *honorable, and right, and pure, and love-*
> *ly, and admirable. Think about things*
> *that are excellent and worthy of praise.*
> **Philippians 4:8 NLT**

Did you catch that? Paul said that you have the power to fix your thoughts on what is holy and will strengthen your mind. This is the power of meditation.

Contrary to what most Christians think when they hear the word *meditation*, this is not a new age concept or a remnant from some ancient pagan religion.

Because of the spiritual stigma that surrounds this concept, many Christians steer clear of it altogether and as a result it's not taught as much as it should be.

Transformation comes, not by making your spirit more powerful, but by renewing your mind.

Meditation is a powerful scriptural principle that results in success and the blessings of God (Joshua 1:8).

When people say, "I can't control the thoughts that pop into my mind," what they're really saying is that they think about the things that randomly present themselves instead of making a plan to think about specific, uplifting things that are found in God's Word.

The results are disastrous.

Uncontrolled thoughts and unguarded minds are

part of the reason that over 33 million Americans (that's over 1 in 10) take antidepressants.[1]

King David gave us a priceless clue when he aptly wrote, "I will not set before my eyes anything that is worthless" (Psalm 101:3).

What you choose to meditate on will either strengthen and guard you or leave you open to the attacks of the enemy.

A PENNY FOR YOUR THOUGHTS

In his ground-breaking book, *Contagious: Why Things Catch On*, Dr. Jonah Berger, professor at the Wharton School of the University of Pennsylvania and an expert on viral marketing, gives us an inside look at what moves people to take action on their thoughts.

After ten years of intense research on subjects like what makes things popular, why people discuss products and ideas, why some stories and rumors are infectious, and what makes online content go viral, he claims to have found the answer.

Obviously, the content of his book is too lengthy to share with you here, but I found something that will help us understand the power of our minds.

He found that observability has a massive impact on the decisions people make.[2] Once we see things, it's impossible to unsee them.

Advertisers know this and do everything in their power to create ad campaigns that you will not only see but remember. By using catchy songs, powerful imagery, and emotional stories (think SPCA commercials with Sarah McLachlan wailing in the background), advertisers invade our minds, plant a seed, and hope it will grow into action.

Satan is the greatest ad executive in the world. He was able to sell specifically forbidden fruit (along with total rebellion) to a man and woman who had no sin in their lives and had daily communion with Almighty God.

The level to which you renew your mind determines the level to which you can activate your faith for God's divine intervention

It just goes to show you how much Solomon understood when he wrote the proverb we discussed earlier in this chapter. (Guard your heart above all else.)

God has given us the power to control and guard our minds so that we can avoid unnecessary pollution and remain filled with faith.

Decide, like King David, that you won't allow worthless, harmful things to harass your mind. Our spiritual lives cannot be any more potent than our minds are renewed. In other words, the level to which you renew your mind determines the level to which you can activate your faith for God's divine intervention.

I'm blessed to come from a family that has built a legacy of ministry. In three generations my family has seen eighteen people serving in ministry with more to come.

As you've read in the few examples I've provided, many of my family have been spared from death, healed of sicknesses and diseases, and protected from accidents.

I've come to realize that none of this is coincidental. The biblical principles that I've shared with you in this book were initiated in our family by my grandparents and passed down through each generation.

These blessings aren't exclusive to the Shuttlesworth family. They are available for all of God's children. They don't randomly appear in the lives of select believers; they are activated by forceful faith.

Will you be the first in your family tree to break the mold of genetic disease and destructive habits? Will you decide this is the last day the enemy will harass your family? Will you make up your mind that your last failure will be your last failure? I believe you will.

Weapons will still be formed against you. The angel of death will still stalk the streets of your neighborhood. But when he sees the blood on your door . . .

He will pass over you.

THE NIGHT THE CHILDREN DIED

"Run!" Adriel screamed at his son. Their calves burned as they sprinted with every last bit of energy in their bodies. "Run toward the blood!"
— Adriel to his son Benjamin

His lungs were burning and every part of his body ached as Adriel approached the entrance to the secret grotto he and his son had discovered.

He could only pray that Benjamin would be there. With the Death Angel's sudden arrival, there was no time for further searching.

He slowly approached the outcropping of rocks that formed the camouflaged cove they had stumbled upon. Although the footing was tricky, they had mastered entering the sanctuary even in the dark.

Adriel came to a halt just before the entrance and inclined his head to listen.

Nothing. Not even the crackling of a fire. He moved forward slowly, strategically placing each step, so as to not make a sound.

Swinging his legs over the edge of the embankment that led down into the sandy banks of the river, he quickly found the familiar footholds and began to lower himself down. His sandals squelched through the damp sand of the riverbank.

He quickly peered into the shallow cave before him. Walking toward the entrance, he cupped his hands over his mouth and shouted in desperation. All inhibition had disappeared as urgency flooded his heart.

"Benjamin, my son, are you here?" He walked closer to the dark mouth of the cave.

There was no response. He felt hot tears run down his cheeks and settle in his beard as he sank to his knees.

Suddenly, he heard rocks shifting inside the cave. More movement. Then a voice.

"Papa?"

"Benjamin?" Adriel said louder than he intended. Benjamin emerged from the cave and ran to his father. Moonlight washed over him as he fell into his kneeling father's arms.

"Benjamin, my Benjamin, my Benjamin," Adriel said in between the kisses he laid upon his son's tear-streaked face. Benjamin's little arms wrapped around Adriel's back tightly.

Adriel winced as the hug renewed the pain in his

back. He realized the pain meant nothing to him now that his son was safely in his arms.

Adriel pulled his son's face from his chest and looked into his eyes. "My son, we must hurry. I have no time to explain. Something terrible is happening tonight and we must get home before it does."

As they reentered through the main gates of the city, Adriel realized things had quickly changed. The streets that were quiet only a half hour ago were now filled with people. Some were weeping and wailing on their knees, others were frantically searching from house to house for missing family members.

It was chaos.

"No! Please, no! Come back to me! My son!" cried a woman to Adriel's left. She lay in the street rocking back and forth with the lifeless body of a boy in her arms.

A chill crept through Adriel's body as he saw the face of the young Egyptian boy whose eyes were frozen open and mouth was hanging agape.

It was as if his last moments were filled with surprise and awe. No blood or wounds were visible on the boy's body. It was as though his heart simply stopped beating.

"Papa, what's going on?" Benjamin's voice was faint and shaky.

"Just keep your eyes on me," Adriel said. "Don't look

at anything but me. We're going home."

Tucking his son close to his body, Adriel pressed his way through the dense crowd that was now filling the main streets of the city.

Adriel noticed eyes turn from sorrow to envy and finally to anger. Why had this Hebrew's son lived when theirs had all died? Some began to hurl vile insults at Adriel and Benjamin as they passed. A few even threw rocks.

Adriel gasped as one of the rocks struck his back, reintroducing him to the severe pain he had suffered earlier in the day. Shouts of protest at the sight of the Hebrew father and son began to fill the air and became progressively louder.

"We must not linger here," Adriel shouted over the din of the crowd. "Hurry!"

They rounded the corner and began to run through the narrow, interconnecting passages and alleys.

The sound of tragedy permeated the air as they delved deeper into the heart of the city.

"Be strong, my son. We're nearly home," Adriel managed. Benjamin could only nod.

"There!" Moonlight flooded from the opening in the alley ahead casting hard shadows on the ground in front of them. "Our house is this way."

With all the strength he could muster, Adriel began

to run as fast as he could, pulling Benjamin close behind him. Once they reached the opening in the alley, their home would be less than two hundred meters away.

They broke into the open and slowed to a brisk walk as the crowd again became too dense to penetrate.

Looking up, Adriel saw the door to their house. Jabari had already applied the blood to the door post. Everything was ready. Then his eyes focused further down the street and he immediately felt sick.

The Death Angel had arrived on their street, about one hundred meters beyond their house. He slowly advanced toward them.

As before, it reached out its hand and touched a door. Moments later muffled screams of grief rang out from inside. *Instant death flowed from its hands.*

Adriel now desperately pushed people out of the way as they pushed down the crowded street. As the way cleared they began to run again.

Suddenly, two figures ran out from an alley onto the street, colliding with Adriel in full force. Adriel and Benjamin fell to the dirt.

It took a moment for Adriel to register what he was seeing as he looked up from the ground. He was so stunned that it may have taken longer—had he not heard the awful sound. *Clink-clink-clink.*

It felt as though his heart stopped beating as he

looked up into the faces of Ammon and his son Odion.

"It cannot be," Ammon growled as Odion was still recognizing the significance of what had happened.

"By the gods, I swear I will kill you this time," Ammon growled.

Odion's eyes filled with a murderous rage as he glared at the man who had humiliated him earlier that day. Bypassing his whip, he grabbed wildly for the curved dagger sheathed on his belt.

"You!" he screamed pointing with his other hand.

Adriel leapt from the ground and grabbed Benjamin. In one swift motion they jumped backwards and hurdled around the two Egyptian taskmasters.

"Run!" Adriel screamed at his son. Their calves burned as they sprinted with every last bit of energy in their bodies. "Run toward the blood!" Adriel shouted to Benjamin.

A quick glance over his shoulder revealed that Ammon and Odion were right behind them. Not realizing his mistake, Adriel tripped and fell in the street.

Odion glided past him in pursuit of Benjamin. Before Adriel could stand to flee again, a heavy kick from Ammon sent him back into the dirt.

He looked up in a daze to see Odion overtake Benjamin knocking him to the ground. He pulled his whip from his belt and began to lash the smaller boy viciously.

The Death Angel was only seventy-five meters beyond them now.

"Jabari!" Adriel screamed as Ammon's strong hands lifted him from the ground. He started to scream again, but Ammon slammed him against the nearest stone building, knocking the wind from his lungs.

Ammon's face was so close to Adriel's that he could feel the hot stench of Ammon's breath on his skin.

"You will not escape me this time," Ammon said. His strong, calloused hands wrapped around Adriel's fragile neck and he began to squeeze.

Jabari, where are you?

Adriel desperately gasped for breath as the Egyptian strangled him, lifting him so high that his feet barely skimmed the ground. His strength was astounding.

Fifty meters away the Death Angel loomed toward them.

Adriel struggled to breathe as his arms flailed wildly. His sight was beginning to darken and he could feel dizziness overtaking him.

Somewhere in the distance he could hear Benjamin crying in the night between each crack of Odion's whip.

Suddenly, light flooded the street as Jabari opened the door to their house. Brandishing his walking stick, he ran shouting into the street toward Odion.

Before Odion could defend himself, Jabari swung a savage blow to his face. There was a crunch as he was sent falling backward into the dust in a daze.

Thirty meters.

Jabari picked Benjamin up and moved him into the house as quickly as possible.

Squeals of breath escaped from Adriel's throat as he tried desperately to breathe. His hands scraped up and down the stone wall behind him searching for something to pull himself away from the giant man. His hand grazed a loose stone in the wall. He clawed at it fiercely, trying to pry it free.

Twenty meters.

Slowly, the stone slid out into the palm of Adriel's hand. He gripped it tightly and drew it back.

Jehovah, help me, he prayed silently.

Gathering every morsel of remaining strength in his being, Adriel swung his arm and connected the stone to Ammon's temple. The blow would certainly have killed a lesser man, but Ammon was immense.

Even so, he dropped Adriel and fell to the ground. Adriel lay in a heap drained of all strength. Gritting his teeth, he grabbed the opening in the wall where the stone had been and pulled himself to his feet.

His legs wobbled as he stumbled toward the door of his house. His head was pounding and he was forced to navigate the street through bloodshot eyes.

He heard the groans of Ammon waking up behind

him. Adriel fell to one knee as Jabari cracked the door open. Benjamin's face peeked out from below.

"Hurry, Adriel! He's coming!" Jabari gestured wildly at Ammon, who was standing to his feet.

Ten meters.

The Death Angel was close enough now that Adriel could have seen his face . . . but he didn't want to. He averted his eyes as he stumbled toward the door.

There was an evil roar from Ammon as he charged toward the frail slave in front of him. Odion sat up from the ground and began to stand.

Jabari reached his arm out the door toward Adriel.

"Take my hand!" he shouted. Adriel collapsed, stretching his arm forward. He felt Jabari's strong grasp as he was pulled through the door and into the house.

Before Jabari could slam the door, Ammon pushed into it with his shoulder. From the floor, Adriel saw Ammon's head quickly turn to the side as he removed his weight from the door. He was looking at something out on the street. He was staring at the Death Angel.

"Who are you?" Adriel heard him say. "Leave my son alone! No! Odion!" The shout was muffled as Jabari quickly shut and barred the door.

"Odion, wake up! WAKE UP!" he pleaded. That's when Ammon began to howl and scream. And then, without warning, the screaming abruptly stopped.

Adriel scrambled to the wall and peered out the window. Ammon and Odion lay dead, piled in a heap in the middle of the street. The dark figure of the Death Angel stood next to them, its arms still outstretched.

As it began to turn back toward the house, Adriel crumpled to the floor and held Benjamin in his arms. Not for the last time that night, tears streamed down his face.

The shadow of the Death Angel fell over the front of their door, blocking the moonlight from their window.

After a moment of contemplation, the Death Angel passed their house and continued down the dark street.

"What's happening?" Benjamin whimpered. "Is that thing coming . . ."

"No, my son. It's leaving. It can't come in."

Benjamin pulled his head from his father's chest revealing a tear-stained face. "It can't? Why?"

"Because," Adriel said, feeling peace for the first time that night. "It saw the blood on the door."

ACKNOWLEDGMENTS

It's so wonderful to have the help and guidance of the Holy Spirit. I constantly thank God for wisdom and revelation from His Word. Truth is freeing (John 8:32). I'd also like to thank:

Carolyn. You're full of faith, love, and grace. You are the best wife I could ask for and the best mom our kids could have. I love you very much.

Madelyn, Brooklyn, and Teddy. The blood will always be on your doors. God's best belongs to you.

Dad and Mom. Thank you for imparting wisdom and revelation and for the endless encouragement.

A.E. and Carlene Shuttlesworth. You both created a family legacy of miracles, signs, and wonders. Your faith has not only carried on through generations, it has increased exponentially.

Stephanie Iaquinto. Aside from the Holy Spirit Who inspires me to write, you are the greatest gift my writing could have ever received. Your vast knowledge of grammar, style, punctuation, and usage never cease to amaze me. You've allowed me to fill your inbox with coal and you've given me back diamonds. Thank you for navigating me through the confusing sections and aiding me where the public school system failed me. We did it again! I thank God for you.

Bishop Rick Thomas. Thank you for believing in this project and making your resources and staff available to me. You live a life of sowing at the highest level.

Barat Knauer. The most grammatically-accurate texter on the planet. Thanks for all the suggestions and for being a manuscript guinea princess.

Sean Thomas. The Darth Vader of design (always killing it). Thank you for using the force to make the artwork shine. Love you, bro!

The maids at various hotels around the country. Thank you for disregarding the do not disturb sign on my door and knocking anyway. You woke me up, but it allowed me to start writing earlier than I planned (Romans 8:28).

NOTES

PREFACE

1. "Transcript of President Bush's Address." CNN. Cable News Network, 21 Sept. 2001. Web. 18 Feb. 2016. <http://edition.cnn.com/2001/US/09/20/gen.bush.transcript/>.

CHAPTER 1: THE DANGER OF CLEAN DOORS

1. Lupkin, Sydney. "Ebola in America: Timeline of the Deadly Virus." *ABC News.* ABC News Network, 17 Nov. 2014. Web. 07 Dec. 2015. <http://abcnews.go.com/Health/ebola-america-timeline/story?id=26159719>.
2. Cuomo, Margaret I. *A World without Cancer: The Making of a New Cure and the Real Promise of Prevention.* New York, NY: Rodale, 2012. Print.
3. Ibid.
4. Oyedepo, David. *Exploits in Ministry.* Ota: Dominion House, 2010. 209. Print.

CHAPTER 2: YOU ARE UNCURSABLE

1. Lake, John G., and Wilford H. Reidt. *Adventures in God.* Tulsa, OK: Harrison House, 1981. Print.
2. Lake, John G., and Roberts Liardon. *John G. Lake: The Complete Collection of His Life Teachings.* Tulsa, OK: Albury Pub., 1999. 443. Print.

CHAPTER 3: THE PROTECTIVE POWER OF DIVINE DIRECTION

1. "Census India." *Census India.* N.p., n.d. Web. 11 Dec. 2015. <http://censusindia.gov.in/Census_Data_2001/Census_Data_Online/Social_and_cultural/Religion.aspx>. On this page, select the "State" radio button, select "Andhra Pradesh" from

the drop-down that appears, and click "Submit". When a new page appears, select the "District" radio button, select "Hyderabad" from the new drop-down, and again click "Submit". The new page displayed is Hyderabad's religious make-up.

CHAPTER 4: THE PROTECTIVE POWER OF PRAYER

1. Hagin, Kenneth E. *Following God's Plan for Your Life*. Tulsa, OK: Faith Library Publications, 1993. 126-128. Print.
2. Shuttlesworth, Ted, Jr. *Praise. Laugh. Repeat.: Living in the Power of Overwhelming Joy*. Virginia Beach: Miracle Word, 2014. 53. Print.
3. Yonggi Cho, David. *Prayer That Brings Revival*. Lake Mary, FL: Creation House, 1998. Print.

CHAPTER 5: THE PROTECTIVE POWER OF FASTING

1. Rodgers, Bob. *101 Reasons to Fast*. Louisville, KY: Bob Rodgers Ministries, 1995. 52. Print.
2. Ibid.
3. Colbert, Don. *Toxic Relief*. Lake Mary, FL: Siloam, 2003. 155. Print.
4. Franklin, Jentezen. *Fasting*. Lake Mary, FL: Charisma House, 2008. 41. Print.
5. Bucholz, Roger, William Fields, and Ursula P. Roach. *20th Century Warriors: Native American Participation in the United States Military*. Washington, D.C.: Dept., 1996. 1-8. *20th Century Warriors: Native American Participation in the United States Military*. CEHP Incorporated, 1996. Web. 19 Dec. 2015. <http://hdl.handle.net/2027/mdp.39015055469772>.
6. Hampton, Bruce. *Children of Grace: The Nez Perce War of 1877*. New York: Henry Holt and Company, 1994, p. 216, 243
7. "Colonel Sanders Story." *Colonel Sanders Story*. Full Gospel Businessmen, n.d. Web. 21 Dec. 2015. <http://fgbt.org/Testimonies/colonel-sanders-story.html>.
8. Wallis, Arthur. *God's Chosen Fast*. Ft. Washington, PA: Christian Literature Crusade, 1968. 50. Print.

CHAPTER 7: THE PROTECTIVE POWER OF YOUR WORDS

1. Clarke, Adam. "Commentary on Mark 11:13". "The Adam Clarke Commentary". http://www.studylight.org/commentaries/acc/view.cgi?bk=40&ch=11. 1832.

CHAPTER 8: THE GATES OF HELL WILL NOT PREVAIL

1. Hagin, Kenneth E. *The Triumphant Church*. Tulsa, OK: RHEMA, 1993. 126-128. Print.

CHAPTER 9: DIVINE PROTECTION FOR YOUR FUTURE

1. Shepherd, R.-M. "Dangerous Consumptions beyond the Grave: Psychic Hotline Addiction for the Lonely Hearts and Grieving Souls." Addiction Research & Theory 17.3 (2009): 278-90. Web.
2. Hitchcock, Mark. "Chapter 10." *The End: A Complete Overview of Bible Prophecy and the End of Days*. Carol Stream: Tyndale House, 2012. N. pag. iBooks. Web. 11 Apr. 2016.
3. Thayer, Joseph. "Ekklesia - New Testament Greek Lexicon - King James Version." *Bible Study Tools*. N.p., n.d. Web. 04 Feb. 2016. <http://www.biblestudytools.com/lexicons/greek/kjv/ekklesia.html>.
4. Pentecost, J. Dwight. *Things to Come: A Study in Biblical Eschatology*. Grand Rapids, MI: Academie, 1964. 262. Print.
5. Thayer, Joseph. "Katecho - New Testament Greek Lexicon - King James Version." *Bible Study Tools.* N.p., n.d. Web. 04 Feb. 2016. <http://www.biblestudytools.com/lexicons/greek/kjv/katecho.html>.

CHAPTER 10: DIVINE PROTECTION FOR YOUR MISSION

1. Cohn, Samuel Kline. The Black Death Transformed: Disease and Culture in Early Renaissance Europe. London: Hodder Education, 2003. 336. Print.
2. Ibid.
3. Lake, John G. "Chapter 12." *The John G. Lake Sermons on Do-*

minion Over Demons, Disease and Death. Ed. Gordon Lindsay. Dallas, TX.: Christ for the Nations, 1980. N. pag. Kindle. Web. 4 Feb. 2016.

4. Lake, John G. Adventures in God. Tulsa, OK: Harrison House, 1991. 80. Print.

5. Lake, John G. "Chapter 12." *The John G. Lake Sermons on Dominion Over Demons, Disease and Death.* Ed. Gordon Lindsay. Dallas, TX.: Christ for the Nations, 1980. N. pag. Kindle. Web. 4 Feb. 2016.

6. Lake, John G. *John G. Lake: The Complete Collection of His Life Teachings.* Comp. Roberts Liardon. Tulsa, OK: Albury Pub., 1999. 15. Print.

7. Sumrall, Lester. "Chapter 11." *The Believer's Handbook.* New Kensington, PA: Whitaker House, 2002. N. pag. Web. 4 Feb. 2016. <https://books.google.com/books?id=hAz2BgAAQBAJ&pg=PT367&lpg=PT367&dq=acts+still+being+written&source=bl&ots=6TYhSngdei&sig=GBz1iAaOMU8XYRDmA-rFVfRSNOs&hl=en&sa=X&ved=0ahUKEwi4j-Oqpd_KAhUGy2MKHV37C5IQ6AEIUDAJ#v=onepage&q=acts%20still%20being%20written&f=false>.

8. "Testimonies." *The Word of Faith* 1 Sept. 2013: 6. Web. 4 Feb. 2016. <https://www.rhema.org/PDFs/WOF/2013SeptWOF.pdf>.

9. "That's My King Dr. S.M. Lockridge - [OFFICIAL]." YouTube. YouTube, n.d. Web. 20 Mar. 2016. <https://www.youtube.com/watch?v=yzqTFNfeDnE>.

10. "Christ for All Nations." *Christ for All Nations.* N.p., n.d. Web. 08 Feb. 2016. <https://new.cfan.org/?office=us>.

11. Clarke, Adam. "Acts 28 Commentary - Adam Clarke Commentary." StudyLight.org. N.p., n.d. Web. 09 Feb. 2016. <http://www.studylight.org/commentaries/acc/view.cgi?bk=43&ch=28>. (Commentary on Acts 28:31).

CHAPTER 11: DIVINE PROTECTION FOR YOUR FAMILY

1. Oyedepo, David O. *Releasing the Supernatural.* Ikeja, Lagos, Nigeria: Dominion House, 1993. 43. Print.

2. Parsley, Rod. *"The Amazing Faith of Smith Wigglesworth."* Ministry Today Magazine. N.p., 30 June 2003. Web. 11 Apr. 2016. <http://ministrytodaymag.com/ministry-today-archives/66-unorganized/7767-the-amazing-faith-of-smith-wigglesworth>.

CHAPTER 12: DIVINE PROTECTION FOR YOUR MIND

1. "Facts & Statistics | Anxiety and Depression Association of America, ADAA." *Anxiety and Depression Association of America, ADAA.* ADAA, n.d. Web. 30 June 2013. <http://www.adaa.org/about-adaa/press-room/facts-statistics>.

2. Berger, Jonah. "Chapter 4." *Contagious: Why Things Catch On.* New York: Simon & Schuster, 2013. N. pag. Print.

ABOUT THE AUTHOR

TED SHUTTLESWORTH JR. has been involved in full-time ministry since he was a child. He began traveling with his father and mother when he was two weeks old. Five years later, in a small church in Northern Maine, Ted felt the call of God on his life.

Ted has been preaching the gospel for close to two decades. As a third-generation minister, the responsibility to reap this end-time harvest of souls has been ingrained in him since childhood.

Ted founded Miracle Word Ministries with a vision to preach the unadulterated gospel and show the miraculous power of Jesus Christ to a hungry generation.

Ted is a graduate of Rhema Bible Training College and currently resides in Virginia Beach, Virginia, with his wife, Carolyn, and their three children.

PRAYER OF SALVATION

Heavenly Father,

Thank you for sending your Son, Jesus, to die for me. I believe that You raised Him from the dead and that He is coming back soon.

I'm asking you to forgive me of my sin and make me brand new. Give me holy desires to pray and read your Word. Empower me by Your Holy Spirit to live for You for the rest of my life.

You are the Lord of my life. I thank you that the old life is gone and a new life has begun, in Jesus Name, Amen.

....

If you prayed this prayer, please contact us. We would like to send you a free gift, pray for you and help you take your next steps in Christ.

info@miracleword.com

YOU MAY HAVE THE FASTEST CAR IN THE WORLD
BUT IF THE GAS TANK IS EMPTY IT'S NOT GOING ANYWHERE

In *Praise. Laugh. Repeat.*, Ted Shuttlesworth Jr. challenges you to discover the power of the overwhelming joy of the Holy Spirit. The Bible tells us that the joy of the Lord is our strength. If the enemy is able to steal your joy he has also stolen your strength and the momentum to do what you've been called to do. You can shed the skin of depression and enter into feather-light living for Jesus Christ beginning today!

The *Praise. Laugh. Repeat. 40-Day Devotional* is specifically designed to be a primer that sets you on a path to the overwhelming joy of Heaven. The amount of spiritual strength you wield is directly connected to the amount of God's Word you've received into your heart.

READ SAMPLE CHAPTERS AND FIND OUT MORE AT
WWW.PRAISELAUGHREPEAT.COM

WATCH OUR VIDEOS ON YOUTUBE

DOWNLOAD OUR FREE APP

CONNECT WITH SOCIAL MEDIA

 @tshuttlesworth

 /MiracleWordMinistries

 Ted Shuttlesworth Jr.

 @tshuttlesworth

 @tedshuttlesworth